A WORKBOOK FOR SELF-STUDY

READING & WRITING FARSI

A Beginner's Guide to the Farsi Script and Language

Pegah Vil and Amir Hossein Ahooie

Mnemonic Illustrations by Jessica Anecito

TUTTLE Publishing

Tokyo │ Rutland, Vermont │ Singapore

Table of Contents

Introduction

How to Use this Book

This book provides a comprehensive guide to fundamentals of the Farsi (Persian) language, covering reading, writing, pronunciation, and basic grammar. No prior knowledge of the language is required. You can learn to read, write, and understand basic Farsi using this book independently, without the need for an instructor. The lessons are easy to understand and are based on proven methods of teaching Farsi to English speakers. This book also includes romanization of the Farsi texts, and mnemonic illustrations to enhance retention.

To learn effectively, you are encouraged to follow the lessons carefully by completing the exercises, and listening to the audio files you can download for free from the Tuttle website. The answers to all exercises are included at the end of the book for reference. In addition, you will be referred to the audio throughout the book regularly.

The questions will be numbered using Arabic numbers (Western digits) unless the answers are in Farsi. In those cases the questions will be numbered using Farsi numbers since the answers will run right to left. See page 14 for an overview of the Farsi numbering system.

An Overview of the Farsi (Persian) Language

Farsi, also known as Persian, is an Iranian language, which belongs to the Indo-European language family. Iranian languages are predominantly spoken in Iran, Afghanistan, Tajikistan, and certain parts of Iraq, Turkey, Syria, Pakistan, China, and the Indian Subcontinent. They include languages such as Farsi, Pashto, Kurdish, etc. Farsi has many dialects spoken in Iran, Afghanistan, and Tajikistan. The Farsi spoken in Afghanistan is known as Dari, and the Farsi of Tajikistan is Tajiki. This book focuses on modern standard Farsi of Iran, also known as Persian-Farsi. Although these dialects sound different, all Farsi dialect speakers can communicate with each other to some extent. While the formal dialects of the language are more similar, the colloquial ones are different.

Colloquial vs. Formal Farsi

Farsi is the official language of Iran and, like any other language, it has many dialects. However, Farsi has two main language styles: colloquial and formal. These styles are significantly different from one another and learners will need to be exposed to both in order to comprehend them. In other words, knowing one style does not guarantee comprehension of the other. Both formal and colloquial Farsi have many registers based on speakers' social class, education, profession, age, etc. This book mainly focuses on formal Farsi as it is more effective for beginning learners to create a strong foundation for learning higher levels.

Formal Farsi

You are more likely to see formal Farsi in written form and the news media, but rather rarely in speaking and conversations. The following traits can be seen in formal Farsi:
- Grammatical and writing rules
- Punctuation
- Complete sentences
- Official and formal vocabulary and sentence structures
- Complete verb forms

Colloquial Farsi

Farsi speakers speak colloquial Farsi, which can be roughly considered as shortened simplified Farsi. Like any other language, colloquial Farsi has various accents and dialects depending on where it is spoken. However, the unofficial standard colloquial Farsi seems to be the Tehrani accent, which is the spoken language of the residents of Tehrna, Iran's capital, and its surrounding areas. The following characteristics are often present in colloquial Farsi:
- Changing and/or shortening sentence structures
- Shortening verbs
- Changing pronunciations
- Using colloquial idioms and slangs
- Using colloquial vocabulary
- Dropping prepositions

In the past colloquial Farsi was not often seen in written form. However, with the advancement of technology and the widespread use of social media, blogs, text messaging, etc., it is becoming more prevalent in writing. So, it seems the borders between formal and colloquial Farsi seem to be fading.

Farsi Writing System

Farsi is typically written using two main scripts: Arabic in Iran and Afghanistan, and Cyrillic in Tajikistan. To make the Arabic script work for Farsi, several letters have been added for the sounds that do not exist in Arabic. The script used in Iran, and the focus of this book, is Arabic (or, in other words, Farsi) script.

Note that only the **script** is Arabic, and the Farsi language is not Arabic, although Farsi text may appear similar to Arabic to those unfamiliar with either language. Arabic is a Semitic language, like Hebrew and Aramaic, and belongs to the Afroasiatic languages, while Farsi is an Iranian language within the Indo-European language group. That said, many Arabic words, clauses, etc. are used in Farsi, and familiarity with Arabic may provide a better understanding of some areas of the Farsi language. Additionally, many educated Farsi speakers know Arabic at various levels ranging from beginner to fluent. Arabic is taught as a second language in schools in Iran from 6th to 12th grade. Overall, the relationship between Arabic and Farsi can be compared to that between Latin and English.

How to Pronounce Farsi

Farsi pronunciation is generally flat. In contrast to a wavy language like English, syllables are is pronounced with the same value. In most English words, one or more syllables are pronounced stronger than the rest. However, this is not the case with Farsi. For most Farsi words, all syllables have the same or similar value when pronounced. To familiarize yourself with this flat pronunciation, listen to audio I-01. In this audio, you will hear the pronunciations of several Farsi words. Listen to them and pay attention to how syllables are pronounced.

salaam: hi   سَلام

daftar: notebook   دَفتَر

medaad: pencil   مِداد

madrese: school   مَدرِسه

How to Write Farsi

Farsi is written from right to left, and books open to the right. Most Farsi letters attach to each other to form words. It can be compared to cursive writing in English, but unlike English, separate letters do not form words. For example, in English, there is **Emma** and *Emma*. They are both written correctly, just in different styles. However, in Farsi detached letters next to each other do not form meaningful words. In other words, there is no way to write in "all caps" in Farsi. Letters need to be attached according to specific attachment rules. Please note that you cannot attach every letter either. Look at these two words. They show how Farsi is written. For detailed information on writing rules, refer to section 2 of this book.

Not Everything Attaches

As noted earlier, Farsi letters need to be attached according to specific rules to form meaningful words. Therefore, there can be words that are completely attached, or made of two or more parts, but they are still considered one word. The space between detached letters of one word is much less than the space between separate words. This is one way to know where a word ends. Another way is through reading and writing practice. As you become more skilled in the language, you will become familiar with the shapes of words, allowing you to know where each word ends. Below are some examples of Farsi words composed of one or more parts:

علی (one word, one part)

رفت (one word, two parts)

می‌خواهم (one word, four parts)

An Overview of Persian Handwriting

Handwriting in Farsi looks quite different from printed text. Similar to formal and colloquial language styles, printed and handwritten scripts differ from each other. Some of the reasons behind this difference include literature, calligraphy, and simplification.

Impact of Calligraphy and Literature

Calligraphy plays an important role in Persian culture. One reason for its significance may be literature and poetry, which has been highly valued among Iranians throughout history.

Before the invention of print, handwriting was the primary means of publishing books. Therefore, the importance of literature may have contributed to making calligraphy, the medium with which literature was presented, significant as well. Another reason was the need for copies of religious texts, such as the Quran after the conversion of Iranians to Islam.

Iran has a long and rich tradition of producing handwritten books that include highly intricate illustrations, illuminations, and calligraphy. These books were created in royal courts by a group of highly skilled artists. Creating books was a group activity with illustrators, calligraphers, and bookbinders working together. Given the amount of work put into making books, sometimes a special book ordered by a king took many years to complete. Many of these books' pages are now in private collections and museums around the world.

Moreover, calligraphy was extensively used in applied arts such as architecture, handicrafts, and textiles for both decorative and practical purposes.

This tradition is still evident today and many Iranians enjoy decorating their homes with works of calligraphy.

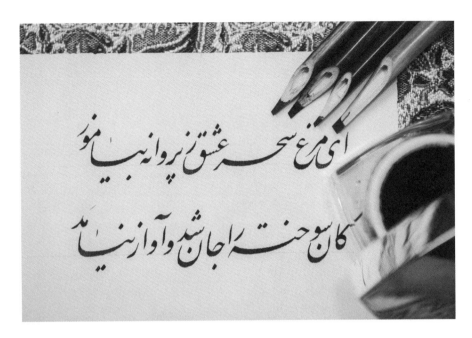

Today, calligraphy and cursive writing are included in the elementary school curriculum in Iran. Thus, the impact of Persian calligraphy is present in most Iranian handwriting. That is one reason why most Farsi handwritten texts look different than printed ones. The other reason for this difference is the frequent presence of dots and teeth in the letters.

ای مرغ سحر عشق ز پروانه بیاموز

کان سوخته را جان شد و آواز نیامد

ای مرغ سحر عشق ز پروانه بیاموز

کان سوخته را جان شد و آواز نیامد

Simplification

Many letters in Farsi have dots and teeth. We cannot simply skip or omit them in handwriting because they change the meaning of what we write. On the other hand, including all of them in handwriting makes writing difficult and time-consuming. To resolve this issue handwriting is simplified. For example, dots can be written as a straight line or an open circle, depending on their number. Look at the image and the text above to see how dots are written. The majority of handwritten texts follow this rule. As mentioned earlier, there are many letters in Farsi that include "teeth." The teeth can also be simplified by skipping them. Look at the words above to see how teeth are skipped. Note that teeth skipping, unlike dot simplification, is considered more of a personal preference than a widely used method. Another way of simplifying handwriting is smoothing the edges and angles. This one is also a personal preference.

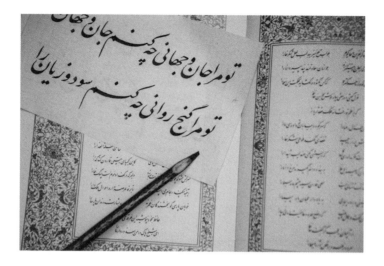

Diacritics

There are diacritics used in Farsi. Diacritics are specific symbols placed on letters that change their behavior. They exist in many languages and serve a variety of functions. In Farsi, most diacritics are short vowels and they help us read the words. Although they may seem to be an essential part of the text, they are not used very often. Diacritics are more likely to be seen in beginner level texts or in words whose pronunciations are thought to be unknown to the reader. Diacritics will be discussed in detail in section 2. This book uses diacritics, but as Farsi learners improve their language skills, they will no longer need them. That is why you will not see diacritics in most Farsi texts.

Sounds That Do Not Exist in English

Farsi includes a few sounds that do not officially exist in English. It is crucial to learn how to pronounce them correctly because being able to pronounce them allows you to read, write, and hear them correctly, as all language skills are interconnected. Learning these sounds may significantly help you improve your Farsi since there are many Farsi words that may sound the same to a native English speaker, but they are in fact different and it can lead to potential confusion. A good example of this issue is a common pronunciation error many native Farsi speakers make as they learn English as a second language. As you will see later in this book, the sound **th** does not exist in Farsi. Therefore, many language learners cannot correctly pronounce this sound. As a result, they cannot differentiate between **t** and **th**. They pronounce **th** as **t**. For a learner with this error "tree" is the same as "three." Now imagine a learner saying something that sounds like "wit." Did they mean "with" or "wit?"

This example illustrates the importance of correct pronunciation. The Farsi sounds that do not exist in English are: **kh**, **zh**, **gh**, and **ein**. These sounds will be discussed in detail in section 2 in addition to the rest of the Farsi alphabet.

The Farsi Alphabet

I n this section the Farsi vowels, consonants, diacritics, and numbers 1–10 are overviewed.

Farsi Vowels

In Farsi there are 3 long and 3 basic short vowels.

Long Vowels

The long vowels have letters in the alphabet. Below are the long vowel and how they sound, as well as a Farsi example for each. Listen to audio A01-01 for the pronunciation of the long vowels and their Farsi examples.

آ   **aa** as in "balm"
آ   as in آب (**aab**: water)

ای   **ee** as in "fleece"
ای   as in ایران (**eeraan**: Iran)

او   **oo** as in "food"
او   as in موش (**moosh**: mouse)

As you can see, the long vowels are written and they have letters assigned to them.

Short Vowels

There are three basic short vowels in Farsi: **a** (ˊ), **e** (ˏ), and **o** (ˈ).

_____   **a** as in "pad"

_____   **a** as in دَر (**dar**: door)

_____   **e** as in "bet"

_____   **e** as in مِس (**mes**: copper)

و

‾‾‾‾‾   o as in "or"

و

‾‾‾‾‾   o as in or سُر (**sor**: slippery)

Listen to audio A01-02 for the pronunciation of the short vowels in the above Farsi examples.

Unlike English, the Farsi short vowels do not have letters in the alphabet. Instead, they are in the form of diacritics that help you read the words. Diacritics are symbols that exist in many languages that make changes to the letters. For example, in French when diacritics are placed on certain letters, they change how the letters are pronounced. In Farsi, most diacritics are placed above or below the letters and add vowels. There are more diacritics in Farsi in addition to the short vowels that will be discussed later in this book.

Consonants

Below are the consonants Farsi shares with English:

b	as in "**b**ed"	**r**	as in "**r**ow"
p	as in "**p**oor"	**sh**	as in "**sh**eep"
t	as in "**t**our"	**f**	as in "**f**ar"
s	as in "**s**ister"	**k**	as in "**c**at"
j	as in "**j**ar"	**g**	as in "**g**uard"
ch	as in "**ch**urch"	**l**	as in "**l**amp"
h	as in "**h**all"	**m**	as in "**m**oon"
d	as in "**d**oor"	**n**	as in "**N**ancy"
z	as in "**z**ebra"	**y**	as in "**y**ellow"

 **Reading Tip**

The **z** and **s** sounds are not interchangeable in Farsi, as they are sometimes in English.

Review of Sounds That Do Not Exist in English

On page 10, we learned that there are several sounds in Farsi that do not exist in English. Listen to audio A01-03 to familiarize yourself with how these sounds are pronounced in simple Farsi words.

kh as in **khaak** (soil)   **gh** as in **ghooree** (teapot)

zh as in **zhaleh** (Persian feminine name)   **ein** as in **ma'bad** (temple)

 **Reading Tip:**

It is important to learn to distinguish these sounds from other similar sounds, as it can affect your listening, speaking, and writing skills. Don't feel intimidated if you cannot tell the difference well at this point. This topic will be discussed in detail in later sections.

Overview of the Farsi Alphabet

The Farsi alphabet comprises 32 letters and like many other languages, there are several letters that sound the same but look different. Review the list of Farsi characters below to learn how they are pronounced. Additionally, listen to audio A01-04 to familiarize yourself with their correct pronunciations.

Farsi Characters	Sound	Farsi Examples
آ	aa	آب (**aab**: water)
ب	b	بابا (**baabaa**: dad)
پ	p	پَر (**par**: feather)
ت – ط	t	تور (**toor**: lace)
ث – س – ص	s	سَر (**sar**: head)
ج	j	جیب (**jeeb**: pocket)
چ	ch	چون (**chon**: because)
ح – ه	h	هیچ (**heech**: nothing)
خ	kh	خاک (**khaak**: soil)
د	d	دور (**door**: far)
ذ – ز – ض – ظ	z	زیر (**zeer**: under)
ر	r	رو (**roo**: on)
ژ	zh	گاراژ (**gaaraazh**: garage)

Farsi Characters	Sound	Farsi Examples
ش	sh	شام (**shaam**: dinner)
ع	ein	سَعید (**sa'eed**: Persian masculine name)
ف	f	کیف (**keef**: purse)
ق – غ	gh	قول (**ghol**: promise)
ک	k	کار (**kaar**: work)
گ	g	گِرد (**gerd**: round)
ل	l	لال (**laal**: mute)
م	m	مَن (**man**: I)
ن	n	نان (**naan**: bread)
و	v	وَلی (**valee**: but)
ی	y	یِک (**yek**: one)

Farsi Numbers

Farsi numbers are written from left to right and follow the same logic as English. The only difference is the characters. As shown below, Farsi digits look different than English. To learn how to write Farsi digits, you'll only need to learn the characters 0 to 9. Then, by placing them next to each other, you can create new numbers. Below are the Farsi numbers 0 to 10.

٠	0	۴	4	۸	8
١	1	۵	5	۹	9
٢	2	۶	6	١٠	10
٣	3	۷	7		

Below are several examples of Farsi numbers and their English equivalents. As you can see, there is no difference other than how they look.

| ۱۰۰ | 100 | | ۸۱ | 81 |
| ۲۰۹۸ | 2,098 | | ۸۷ | 87 |

 ## Writing Rules

Trace the numbers following the writing instruction of each number.

Reading Numbers

Reading Farsi numbers shares the same logic as English. The names of the numbers 1 to 20 need to be memorized. For numbers larger than 20, you only need to know how to say the ones, the tens, the hundreds, the thousands, etc.

Listen to audio A01-05 to familiarize yourself with the pronunciations of Farsi numbers 0 to 10.

0	۰ (sefr)	6	۶ (shesh)
1	۱ (yek)	7	۷ (haft)
2	۲ (do)	8	۸ (hasht)
3	۳ (se)	9	۹ (noh)
4	۴ (chaahaar)	10	۱۰ (dah)
5	۵ (panj)		

Just reading the romanized pronunciations is not an effective way of learning to pronounce Farsi words correctly. I encourage you to listen to the audio files when the book references them. The romanized pronunciations are included as an aid. Listening to the audio may help train your ear to better understand spoken Farsi, as well as help you read and pronounce Farsi correctly.

Exercise 1.1   Listen to audio A01-06 and select the correct number you hear.

1. A – ۵   B – ۶   2.   A – ۲   B – ۰
    C – ۹   D – ۳   C – ۶   D – ۸

3. A – ۷   B – ۸   4.   A – ۳   B – ۱
    C – ۴   D – ۶   C – ۵   D – ۸

5. A – ۰   B – ۲   6.   A – ۵   B – ۴
    C – ۹   D – ۷   C – ۱   D – ۸

Exercise 1.2   Listen to audio A01-07 and transcribe the numbers you hear in Farsi digits.

1. _____   2.   _____

3. _____   4.   _____

5. _____   6.   _____

7. _____   8.   _____

9 . _____   10. _____

Reading and Writing the Farsi Alphabet

There are 32 letters in the Farsi alphabet, which is called **Alefbaa**. In addition, there are 3 basic diacritics (short vowels) that are not included in the alphabet, which we will discuss along with the letters, as well as a few additional diacritics. Upon completing this section, you will be able to read and write Farsi. You will also learn some Farsi words and sentences. Below is the list of all Farsi letters and their different forms, in the order they appear in the alphabet. Note that the book will discuss the letters in a different order, based on letter use frequency in the Farsi language. Listen to audio A02-01 for the pronunciations of the letters and their names.

Alefbaa	Sound	Name
ا آ	aa	alef
ب ب	b	be
پ پ	p	pe
ت ت	t	te
ث ث	s	se
ج ج	j	jeem
چ چ	ch	che
ح ح	h	he
خ خ	kh	khe
د	d	daal
ذ	z	zaal
ر	r	re

Alefbaa	Sound	Name
ز	z	ze
ژ	zhe	zhe
س س	s	seen
ش ش	sh	sheen
ص ص	s	saad
ض ض	z	zaad
ط	t	taa
ظ	z	zaa
ع ع ع ع	'e	ein
غ غ غ غ	gh	ghein
ف ف	f	fe
ق ق	gh	ghaaf

Alefbaa	Sound	Name
کک ک	k	kaaf
گگ گ	g	gaaf
لـ ل	l	laam
مـ م	m	meem

Alefbaa	Sound	Name
نـ ن	n	noon
و	v	vaav
ه هـ ـهـ ـه	h	he
یـ ی	y	ye

As you can see, there are several letters that look different but sound the same. Keep in mind that only knowing the sounds is not enough to write Farsi correctly. For example, you need to know which **s** or **z** sounding letter needs to be used in a certain word. While there is no set rule for this, as you learn the alphabet and new words, you will begin to figure it out, and after some practice, you will automatically use the correct letters. Similarly, in English, there are so many words that you need to be familiar with their spelling to be able to write them correctly, as they do not follow general spelling rules. This is especially evident in words of foreign origin used in English. One reason that there are many letters with the same sound in Farsi is because of borrowed words from other languages, especially Arabic. In these instances, we tend to use the original spellings or make minimal modifications to them.

THE FARSI ALPHABET

ا آ **Alef**
(aa)

army

آ is the first and most frequently used letter in Farsi. It sounds like **a** in the English word *army*. آ has 2 forms of initial and medial/final. As you heard in audio A02-01, the name of this letter is **alef**.

 Writing Rules

آ   Initial form is only used at the beginning of the word and does not attach.

ا   Medial/final form is used in the middle or end as the name suggests. It attaches to the right to the letters that attach to the left.

Writing Tip:

In Farsi the letter that comes before/on the right determines the attachment. There are exceptions to this, but it generally applies. Follow the steps below to write آ and ا. Write them several times in the designated space. Note that unlike most diacritics, writing the "hat"—as we call it کلاه (**kolaah:** *hat*) in Farsi—on top of the initial آ is mandatory.

(aa)

Listen to audio A02-02 to familiarize yourself with the pronunciation of آ in a basic Farsi word.

آ **aa** آب – **aab** (water)

Now practice writing the word آب a few times following the steps below.

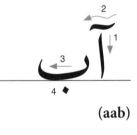

(aab)

 Reading Tip:

Note that the medial/final form of ا can be used at the beginning of the word, but it will sound different, which will be reviewed later in this section. This is why including the "hat" in the initial آ is important.

Exercise 2.1   Look at the text below and circle all instances of ا / آ.

اِمروز دَر آبادان بارانِ سِیل آسایی بارید. مَردُم شَهر را تَخلیه کَردَند وَ به سوی شَهرهایِ مُجاوِر فَرار کَردَند.

ب ‍ب‍ ﺑ **Be (b)**

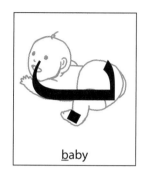

baby

ب sounds like **b** in the English word *baby*. This letter has two forms of initial/medial and final. The letter's name is **be**, as you heard in audio A02-01.

 Writing Rules

ﺑ   Initial/medial form attaches on both sides.

ب   Final form attaches on the right to the letters that attach on the left.

Follow the steps below to write ب. Write it several times in the designated space.

(b)

Listen to audio A02-03 to familiarize yourself with the pronunciation of ب in a basic Farsi word.

ب   **b**   بابا – **baabaa** (dad)

Now practice writing the word بابا a few times while paying attention to the order shown below.

(baabaa)

Exercise 2.2 Look at the text below and circle all instances of ب.

بَرایِ مُوَفَقیَّت دَر دَبِستان وَ تَحصیلاتِ اِبتِدایی بایَد پِدَر وَ مادَر نَقشِ فَعّالی دَر مَدرِسهیِ

بَچّه داشته باشَند.

Exercise 2.3 Listen to audio A02-04 and complete the words below.

٢. ب ____ با   ١. ____ ب

۴. ____ اب   ٣. ا ____

ن ـن ن **Noon**
(n)

necklace

ن sounds like **n** in the English word *necklace*. It has two forms of initial/media and final. As you heard in the audio A02-01, this is called **noon**.

✎ Writing Rules

ـنـ Initial/medial form attaches on both sides.
ن Final form attaches on the right of the letters that attach on the left.

Follow the steps below to write ن. Write it several times in the designated space.

(n)

Listen to audio A02-05 to get familiar with the pronunciation of ن in a Farsi word.

ن   **n**   نان – **naan** (bread)

(naan)

Writing Tip:

As you may have noticed, a general rule for writing is that you write parts of the attached letters first, then place the dots for that section before you move on to the next. This approach makes writing easier and reduces the likelihood of skipping or misplacing the dots. As stated earlier, using dots correctly is important, as not using so can alter the meanings.

Exercise 2.4   Look at the text below and circle all instances of ن.

اَنار که روزگاری فَقَط دَر خاوَرمیانه و مِدیتَرانه شِناخته شُده بود، اِمروزه دَر اَکثَر مَناطِقِ دُنیا به فُروش می‌رِسَد.

Exercise 2.5   Attach the following letters according to the writing rules to form meaningful words then write them in the designated space.

۱.   ن + ا + ن = _____

۲.   ب + ا + ب + ا = _____

۳.   آ + ن = _____

Exercise 2.6   Listen to the audio A02-06 and complete the words below.

۱. ___ان   ۲. نـ ___ب

۳. ___ا___آ   ۴. ___ ن

د Daal (d)

drum

د sounds like **d** in the English word *drum.* Its name is **daal**, as you heard in audio A02-01. د has only one form and attaches on the right.

✎ Writing Rules

د Initial/medial/final attaches to the right side of letters that attach on the left. Like other letters, its attachment is dependent on the letter that comes before it.

Follow the steps below to write د. Write it several times in the designated space.

(d)

Listen to audio A02-07 to familiarize yourself with the pronunciation of باد.

باد – **baad** (wind)

Now write the word باد several times following the steps shown.

(baad)

Exercise 2.7 Look at the text below and circle all instances of د.

دَروازهیِ مِلَل دَر تَختِ جَمشید سازه‌ای سَنگی وَ بسیار عَظیم اَست. رویِ آن حیواناتِ اُسطوره‌ای کَنده کاری شده، که وَظیفه‌یِ پاسداری اَز ساختمان را بَرعُهده دارَند.

Exercise 2.8   Listen to audio A02-08 and fill in the blanks.

٣. د —غ   ٢. —ر   ١. —ار

٦. فرد —   ٥. —را—ر   ٤. دَروـزه

٨. —با—   ٧. —اد

Exercise 2.9   Fill in the blanks using د.

٣. —ارا   ٢. —ا—   ١. —ارو

٥. —اَرَ—   ٤. —ر َ—

ر **Re**
(**r**)

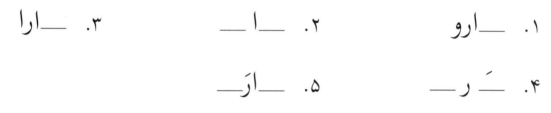

rabbit

ر sounds similar to **r** in the English word *rabbit*, but a little flatter in pronunciation. Listen to audio A02-09 to become familiar with the correct pronunciation of **r** in a Farsi word. Pay attention to the flatness of ر and how it differs from the English **r**.

ر   **r**   بَرادَر – **baraadar** (brother)

 **Writing Rules**

ر Initial/medial/final attaches on the right. Its attachment is dependent on the letter that comes before it.

Follow the steps below to write ر. Write it several times in the designated space.

(r)

Listen to audio A02-10 to get familiar with a couple of Farsi words using ر.

ر آرد – **aard** (flour)

ر باران – **baaraan** (rain)

Now practice writing these words in the space below following the steps shown.

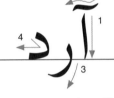

(aard)

(baaraan)

Exercise 2.10 Look at the text below and circle all instances of ر.

روزی روزگاری مَردی دَر شَهری زِندِگی می‌کَرد. یک روز شِنید که ماهیِ بُزُرگی اَز رودخانه صِید شُده که دَر شِکَمَش یک سَنگِ گِرانبَها اَست.

Exercise 2.11   Listen to audio A02-11 and fill in the blanks.

٣. ‌__ا__   ٢. __اد__   ١. ان__ا__ان

٦. دَ __   ٥. أَن __ __ __   ٤. __ __ ن

٧. آ__ __

Exercise 2.12   Listen to audio A02-12 and transcribe it.

٢. ——————————   ١. ——————————

٤. ——————————   ٣. ——————————

٦. ——————————   ٥. ——————————

A ا_َ

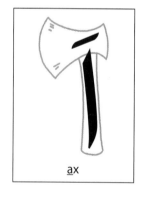

ax

ا sounds like **a** in the English word *ax*, as briefly mentioned before. ا is not an official letter of the alphabet, but a short vowel that takes the form of ا in the beginning of the word and becomes a diacritic everywhere else. The reason for adding the ا at the beginning is that diacritics need a letter to be placed on and you cannot use them standalone. When you see ـَ on top of a letter, it means you read it with the short vowel **a**.

Look at the word below and try to read it.

در

As you can see, there are two consonants in the word and it is not easy to read. But when you add ـَ on top of د, it tells you to read the د with the ـَ vowel. So the complete form of the word is:

دَر – **dar** (door)

Listen to audio A02-13 to familiarize yourself with the pronunciation of دَر.

Writing Rules

ا Initial does not attach.

ـَ Medial is placed on top of letters to add the vowel **a**.

Follow the steps below to write اٗ. Write both forms several times in the designated space.

(a)

Listen to audio A02-14 to become familiar with the pronunciation of ـَ in a simple Farsi word.

اَ **a** اَنار – **anaar** (pomegranate)

Now practice writing it in the designated space below.

(anaar)

 Writing Tip:

Note that writing the non-initial form of ــَـ is not mandatory, as well as the other short vowels. The ا part, however, is mandatory in the initial آ form. For example, in the word أنار (**anaar**: pomegranate) writing the ا is mandatory, but the ــَـ diacritic is not. As learners become more skilled in reading and writing, the use of diacritics gradually decreases until they are no longer used. In general, diacritics are primarily used for beginner learners and also for some low-frequency or unfamiliar words to assist with proper pronunciation.

Exercise 2.13   Look at the text below and circle all instances of ــِـ.

مُوَفَقِیَت تَحصیلی به مَوارِدِ بِسیاری بَستِگی دارَد: اَز جُمله میزانِ تَلاشِ دانِش آموز و کیفیَتِ کُتُبِ دَرسی. اَلبَته نَقشِ مُعَلِم را نِمی‌توان نادیده گِرِفت.

Exercise 2.14   Attach each group of letters according to the writing rules to form meaningful words. Then write them in the designated space.

۱.   د + ــَـ + ن + د + ا + ن = _____

۲.   ب + ــَـ + د = _____

۳.   اَ + ن + ا + ر = _____

۴.   اَ + ب + ر = _____

Exercise 2.15   Listen to audio A02-15 and fill in the blanks.

٣. ن ــ دان   ٢. ــ ندا ــ   ١. ــ بــ ــ

                     ٥. ــ ربــ ن   ٤. ــ ر ــ

Exercise 2.16   Listen to audio A02-16 and transcribe it.

٢. _____   ١. _____

٤. _____   ٣. _____

م مــ **Meem**
(m)

milk

م sounds just like **m** in the English word *milk*. Its name is **meem** in the alphabet as you heard in audio A02-01. م has two forms of initial/medial and final attached/detached.

✎ **Writing Rules**

مـ   Initial/medial, attached on both sides to the letters that attach.

م   Final attached/detached, attaches on the right to the letters that attach on the left.

Look at the image below and follow the steps to write م. Write it several times in the designated space.

(m)

Listen to audio A02-17 to get familiar with the pronunciation of م in a Farsi word.

م **m** مادَر – **maadar** (mother)

Now practice writing مادَر several times below. Try to follow the instruction.

(maadar)

Exercise 2.17 Look at the text below and circle all instances of م.

به گُزارِشِ خَبَرگُزاریِ میراثِ فَرهَنگی بیش اَز ۱۵۰۰ نَفَر اَز مَردُمِ شَهرهایِ مُجاوِر بَرایِ

کُمَک به زِلزِله‌زَدِگان به سویِ بَم حَرِکَت کَردَند، وَلی به دَلیلِ بَسته بودَنِ جادّه‌ها مُوَفَّق

نَشُدَند به شَهر بِرِسَند.

Exercise 2.18 Complete the following.

‏۱. م + ﹷ + ر + د = ـــــــــــــــــــــــــــــــ

‏۲. د + ا + م + ﹷ + ن = ـــــــــــــــــــــــــــــــ

‏۳. م + ا + م + ا + ن = ـــــــــــــــــــــــــــــــ

‏۴. د + ا + م = ـــــــــــــــــــــــــــــــ

Exercise 2.19   Listen to audio A02-18 and transcribe it.

_____ .٢   _____ .١

_____ .۴   _____ .٣

                                    _____ .۵

Seen سـ ـس ـسـ س
(s)

soup

س sounds like **s** in the English word *soup*. س is called **seen** in the alphabet as you heard in audio A02-01. It has two forms of initial/medial and final detached/attached.

 Writing Tip:

There are several letters in Farsi that sound like **s**, but they are not interchangeable in spelling, even though they sound identical. As you learn new words, it is important to pay attention to their specific spellings. Additionally, the **s** and **z** sounds are not interchangeable in Farsi, as they sometimes are in English.

 Writing Rules
ـسـ   Initial/medial attaches on both sides.
س   Initial/medial attaches on both sides.

Follow the steps below to write س. Write both forms several times in the designated space.

(s)

Listen to audio A02-19 to get familiar with the pronunciation of س in a Farsi word.

س **s** سَبَد – **sabad** (basket)

Now try writing the word سَبَد several times.

(sabad)

Exercise 2.20   Complete the following.

١ . س + ـَـ + ب + ـَـ + د = _____

٢ . س + ـَـ + ر = _____

٣ . س + ر + ا + ر + ا = _____

۴ . س + ـَـ + ر + م + ا = _____

Exercise 2.21   Listen to audio A02-20 and fill in the blanks.

١ . أ__ب   ٢ . آ__د__م__

٣ . د __ __

Exercise 2.22 Listen to audio A02-21 and transcribe it.

_____ ٢.   _____ ١.

_____ ۴.   _____ ٣.

ت ـت ـ **Te**
(t)

tiger

ت sounds like **t** in the English word *tiger*. ت is called **te** in the alphabet as you heard in audio A02-01. As previously discussed, there are several letters in Farsi that sound like **t**. When you learn words with the **t** sound, pay attention to the type of **t** used. ت has two forms of initial/medial and final detached/attached.

 Writing Rules

ـتـ   Initial/medial attaches on both sides.

ـت   Final detached/attached attaches on the right.

And again its attachment is determined by the letter that comes before it. Look at the image below and follow the steps to write ت. Write it several times in the designated space.

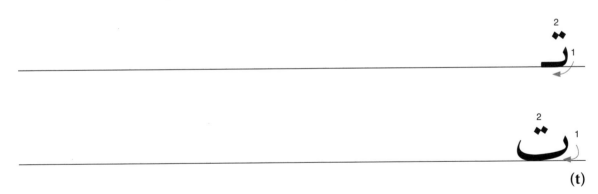

(t)

 **Writing Tip:**

As you learn new letters, pay attention to their details, such as dots and teeth. ت has two dots. You can either write it either with the 2 dots or with a short horizontal line in place of the dots for ease and speed of writing. This can also be applied to all the letters with two dots.

تـ ـتـ

Listen to audio A02-22 to get familiar with the pronunciation of ت in two Farsi words.

ت   t   دَست – **dast** (hand and arm)

ت   n   تاب – **taab** (swing)

Now practice writing دَست and تاب several times below. Try to follow the steps.

(dast)

(taab)

Exercise 2.23   Complete the following words.

۱.   ت + ا + ب = _____

۲.   د + ـَ + س + ت = _____

۳.   ت + ـَ + م + ا + س = _____

۴.   م + ا + س + ت = _____

Exercise 2.24 Listen to audio A02-23 and fill in the blanks.

٢. ـــــ بـَ ـــــ   ١. بادـــم

٤. ـــــ بَ   ٣. ـــــ رس

Exercise 2.25 Listen to audio A02-24 and transcribe it.

٢. _____   ١. _____

٤. _____   ٣. _____

ز **Ze**
(z)

zebra

ز sounds like the **z** in the English word *zebra*. ز is called **ze** in the alphabet as you heard in audio A02-01. As may you have noticed, there are several letters in the Farsi alphabet that sound identically like the letter **z**. Pay attention to the new words you learn and the type of **z** they use. ز has only one form with the same writing rules as ر and د.

✎ Writing Rules

ز Initial/medial/final attaches on the right.

Look at the image below and follow the steps to write ز. Write it several times in the designated space. Make sure you include the dot.

(z)

Listen to audio A02-25 to become familiar with the pronunciation of **z** in two Farsi words.

ز   **z**   سَبز – **sabz** (green)

ز   **z**   زَرد – **zard** (yellow)

Now practice writing سَبز and زَرد several times below. Try to follow the steps.

سَبز

(sabz)

زَرد

(zard)

Exercise 2.26   Complete the following.

١.   ز + ــَ + ر = _____

٢.   ز + ــَ + ن = _____

٣.   ز + ــَ + ر + د = _____

۴.   ز + ــَ + ب + ا + ن = _____

Exercise 2.27   Listen to audio A02-26 and fill in the blanks.

١.   سَـ ___ ___ ___   ٢.   بـ ___ زا ___

٣.   ___ مان   ۴.   سَـ ___ با ___

Exercise 2.28 Listen to audio A02-27 and transcribe it.

_____ .۲   _____ .۱

_____ .۴   _____ .۳

 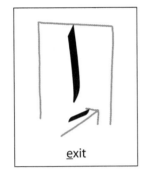

ا sounds like **e** in the English word *exit*. Just like آ, it is written as ا if the word starts with ا. When you see ‗ under a letter, you need to read it with the short vowel **e**.

Reading Tip:

In English **e** sometimes sounds like *i* (for example in *be*). However, in Farsi it sounds only like ا (**e**). ا follows most of the آ rules. The exception in ا is that it becomes a letter when it is at the end of the word.

Writing Rules

  Initial does not attach to anything, written standalone. This form is only used if the word starts with ا (**e**).

‗ Medial is a non-mandatory diacritic.

ﻪ Final attached.

ه Final detached.

Writing Tip:

In Farsi, writing short vowel diacritics are not mandatory but they are included in this book to facilitate reading. The final forms of ‗ however, are mandatory, as they become a letter. There are many words in Farsi that end with this letter.

Look at the image below and follow the steps to write ا. Write it several times in the designated space.

(e)

Now listen to audio A02-28 to get familiar with the pronunciation of ا in several Farsi words.

ا	e	اِداره	–	**edaare** (office)
ـ	e	مِداد	–	**medaad** (pencil)
ـه	e	مَدرِسه	–	**madrese** (school)
ه	e	تازه	–	**taaze** (fresh)

Practice writing what you heard in the audio several times following the steps below.

(edaare)

(medaad)

(madrese)

(taaze)

Exercise 2.29 Complete the words below.

١. _____ = ر + ب + ــِ + ز

٢. _____ = ن + ا + ت + ــِ + ب + ــَ + د

٣. _____ = ر + ــِ + د + ا + ن

۴. _____ = ه + س + ــِ + ر + د + ــَ + م

۵. _____ = ه + ر + ا + ت + ــِ + س

Exercise 2.30 Listen to audio A02-29 and fill in the blanks.

١. ما__ ٢. نَ__رد__ ٣. دَ__ست__ن

۴. داد__ ۵. تا __ __

Exercise 2.31   Listen to audio A02-30 and transcribe it.

_____ .٢   _____ .١

_____ .۴   _____ .٣

ک ک Kaaf
(k)

cat

ک sounds like **k** in the English word *cat*. ک is called **kaaf** in the alphabet as you heard in audio A02-01. It has two forms of initial/medial and final detached/attached.

✎ **Writing Rules**
ک   Initial/medial attaches on both sides.
ک   Final detached/attached attaches on the right.

Look at the image below and follow the steps to write ک. Write it several times in the designated space.

(k)

Now listen to audio A02-31 to get familiar with the pronunciation of ک in several Farsi words.

ک   **k**   کار – **kaar** (work)
ک   **k**   نَمَک – **namak** (salt)

Practice writing what you heard in the audio several times and try to follow the steps.

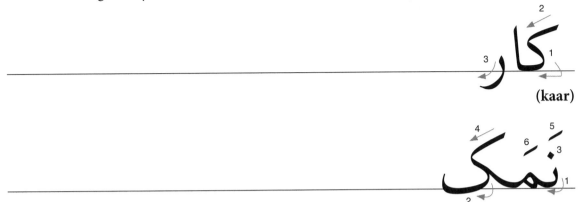

(kaar)

(namak)

Exercise 2.32 Complete the following.

$$ ۱. \quad \underline{\hspace{4cm}} = ب + ا + ت + \_ + ک $$

$$ ۲. \quad \underline{\hspace{4cm}} = م + \_ + ک $$

$$ ۳. \quad \underline{\hspace{4cm}} = ک + ن + ا + ب $$

$$ ۴. \quad \underline{\hspace{4cm}} = س + ا + ن + \_ + ک + س + اِ $$

Exercise 2.33 Listen to audio A02-32 and fill in the blanks.

$$ ۱. \quad ت\_\_ا\_\_ \qquad\qquad ۲. \quad \_\_اس\_\_ $$

$$ ۳. \quad مَس \_\_ ن \qquad\qquad ۴. \quad ن\_\_ تِ \_\_ $$

Exercise 2.34   Listen to audio A02-33 and transcribe it.

_____ ٢.   _____ ١.

_____ ٤.   _____ ٣.

اي يـ ى **Ee**  ای, unlike its appearance, is a long vowel. It sounds like *i* (**ee**) in the English word *bee*. Being a long vowel, it is not included in the alphabet. It has three forms of initial, medial, and final.

bee

 ## Writing Rules

ايـ | ا   Initial, attaches on the left. This form is used when a word starts with the sound *ee*.
ـيـ   Medial, attaches on both sides.
ى   Final detached/attached, attaches on the right.

Look at the image below and follow the steps to write ای. Write it several times in the designated space.

(ee)

Now listen to audio A02-34 to get familiar with the sound of ای in several Farsi words.

ا ایـ   **i**   ایران   – **eeraan** (Iran)

یـ   **i**   سیب   – **seeb** (apple)

ی   **i**   آبی   – **aabee** (blue)

Practice writing what you heard in the audio several times and try to follow the steps.

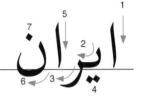

(eeraan)

(seeb)

(aabee)

 Writing Tip:

You can write the ایـ dots as a straight line to simplify writing like the image below.

ایـ

Exercise 2.35   Complete the following.

۱. م + ی + ن + ا = ــــــــــــــ

۲. س + ی + ر = ــــــــــــــ

۳. س + ی + ن + ی = ــــــــــــــ

۴. ز + ی + ر = ــــــــــــــ

Exercise 2.36   Listen to audio A02-35 and fill in the blanks.

۲. ــ ــــ ــرانــ   ۱. ــ مــ ذ ــ

۴. ــ ــ ســ   ۳. ر ــ ــ

Exercise 2.37   Listen to audio A02-36 and transcribe it.

۲. ــــــــــــــ   ۱. ــــــــــــــ

۴. ــــــــــــــ   ۳. ــــــــــــــ

ی یـ ی **Ye**
(y)

yarn

ی looks almost the same as ای, but sounds different. ی sounds like **y** in *yarn*. It is a consonant, unlike ای, which is a long vowel. ی is the alphabet's last letter and it is called *ye*, as you heard in the audio A02-01.

 **Reading Tip:**

This is how you differentiate between ای and ی:

1. If the word starts with ﯾ, then it is **y**. But if it starts with اﯾ, it is **ee**.
2. If there are diacritics on the medial and final ﯾs, it is **y**, as we do not normally place diacritics on a long vowel (ای).

Again, reading and writing practice is the best way to acquire the skill to differentiate between these two sounds.

 ## Writing Rules

ﯾ Initial/medial attaches on both sides.

ی Final detached/attached attaches on the right.

Look below and follow the steps to write ی. Write it several times in the designated space.

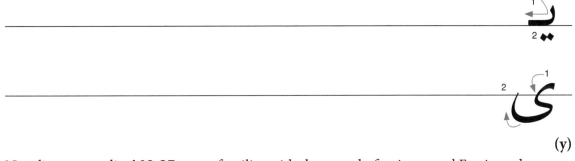

(y)

Now listen to audio A02-37 to get familiar with the sound of ی in several Farsi words.

ﯾ y سایه – **saaye** (shadow)

ﯾ y دَریا – **daryaa** (sea)

Practice writing what you heard in the audio several times and try to follow the steps.

(saaye)

(daryaa)

Exercise 2.38 Complete the following.

١. ـَـ + ی + ـَـ + ز + د = _____

٢. ی + ـِـ + ن = _____

٣. س + ا + ی + ه = _____

۴. آ + ر + ی + ا = _____

Exercise 2.39 Listen to audio A02-38 and fill in the blanks.

١. سِ ـــ ل   ٢. ـــ نِ ـــ

٣. ـــ ـــ س   ۴. دَ ـــ ـــ ا

Exercise 2.40 Listen to audio A02-39 and transcribe it.

١. _____   ٢. _____

٣. _____

Exercise 2.41 Listen to audio A02-40 and write ی (**y**) or ای (**ee**) as you hear them.

_____ ۲.   _____ ۱.

_____ ۴.   _____ ۳.

او و **Oo**

food

او sounds like **oo** in the English word *food*. It has two forms of initial and medial/final. Like other long vowels, او is not a formal alphabet letter.

 Writing Rules

او   Initial does not attach.

و   medial/final attaches on the right to the letter before it if that letter attaches on the left.

Look below and follow the steps to write او. Write it several times in the designated space.

(oo)

Now listen to audio A02-41 to get familiar with the sound of او‏ا in several Farsi words.

مو   –   **oo**   و   **moo** (hair)

زود   –   **oo**   و   **zood** (early)

کبوتَر   –   **oo**   و   **kabootar** (pigeon)

Practice writing what you heard in the audio several times following the steps below.

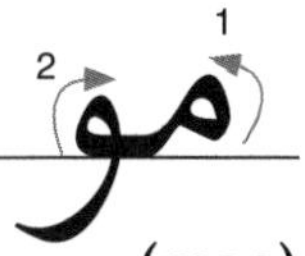

موْ

(moo)

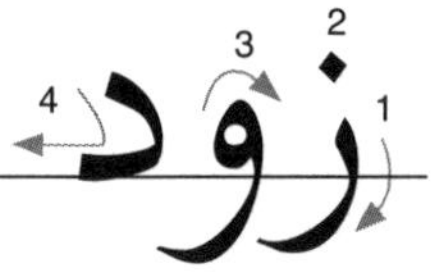

زوْد

(zood)

کبوتَر

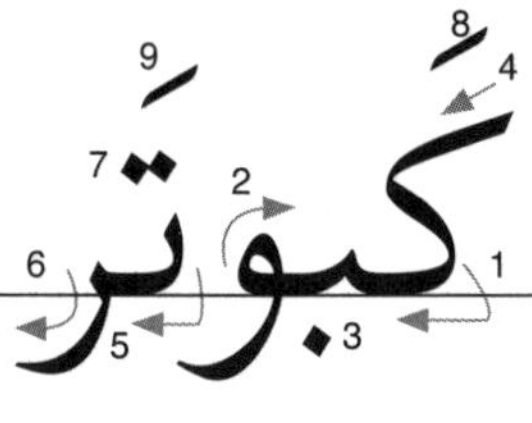

(kabootar)

Exercise 2.42   Complete the following.

١ .   س + و + د = _____

٢ .   ب + و + د = _____

٣ .   د + و + ز + ‒́ + ن + د + ه = _____

Exercise 2.43 Listen to audio A02-42 and fill in the blanks.

۲. ر——ن———   ۱. سـ——زَ——

۴. د——ر——   ۳. ——کَبـ——

Exercise 2.44 Listen to audio A02-43 and transcribe it.

۳. ———————   ۲. ———————   ۱. ———————

۵. ———————   ۴. ———————

پ پ پ **Pe**
(p)

pumpkin

پ sounds like **p** in *pumpkin*. It has two forms of initial/medial and final detached/attached. پ is called **pe** in the alphabet as you heard in audio A02-01.

 ### Writing Rules

پ Initial/medial attaches on both sides.
پ Final detached/attached attaches on the right, depending on the letter before it if that letter attaches on the left.

Look at the image below and follow the steps to write پ. Write it several times in the designated space.

(p)

 Writing Tip:

Like all letters with more than one dot, you can simplify the dots like below. The symbol for three dots is an open circle.

Now listen to audio A02-44 to get familiar with the sound of پ in several Farsi words.

پ   **p**   پا – **paa** (foot and leg)

پ   **p**   پِدَر – **pedar** (father)

Practice writing what you heard in the audio several times and try to follow the steps below.

(paa)

(pedar)

Exercise 2.45 Complete the following.

۱. ‏پ + و + ن + ه = _____

۲. ‏پ + ِ + د + َ + ر = _____

۳. ‏پ + َ + ت + و = _____

Exercise 2.46 Listen to audio A02-45 and fill in the blanks.

۱. ‏__وست   ۲. ‏__ __ ر

۳. ‏__نـ__ __   ۴. ‏__و__

Exercise 2.47 Listen to audio A02-46 and transcribe it.

۱. _____   ۲. _____

۳. _____   ۴. _____

شـ ش Sheen (s)

shark

ش sounds like **sh** in the word *shark*. As you heard in audio A02-01, its name is **sheen** in the Farsi alphabet. It has two forms of initial/medial and final detached/attached, following the same rules as س.

Writing Rules

شـ   Initial/medial attaches on both sides.

ش   Final detached/attached attaches on the right to the letters that attach on the left.

Follow the steps below to write ش. Write it several times in the designated space.

(sh)

 Writing Tip:

Like other three-dot letters, you can simplify the ش dots with an open circle instead of the three dots.

Now listen to audio A02-47 to get familiar with the sound of ش in several Farsi words.

شـ	**sh**	شور	–	**shoor** (salty)
شـ	**sh**	شام	–	**shaam** (dinner)
ش	**sh**	آش	–	**aash** (Persian soup)

Practice writing what you heard in the audio several times and try to follow the steps.

(shoor)

(shaam)

(aash)

Exercise 2.48   Complete the following.

۱.   ش + و+ ش = _____

۲.   ش + ــَ + م + ش + ی + ر = _____

۳.   ش + ا + ن + ه = _____

Exercise 2.49   Listen to audio A02-48 and fill in the blanks.

۱.   ____انس   ۲.   ____و____تَر   ۳.   شِ____

Exercise 2.50   Listen to audio A02-49 and transcribe it.

۱.   _____   ۲.   _____

Fe ف ف
(f)

fish

ف sounds like **f** in the English word *fish*. It is called **fe** in the Farsi alphabet as you heard in audio A02-01. It has two forms of initial/medial and final detached/attached.

 Writing Rules

ف Initial/medial attaches on both sides.

ف Final detached/attached attaches on the right to the letters that attach on the left.

Look at the image below and follow the steps to write ف. Write it several times in the designated space.

_____

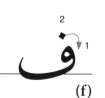

_____

(f)

Now listen to audio A02-50 to get familiar with the sound of ف in several Farsi words.

ف   **f**   کیف – **keef** (purse)

ف   **f**   فارسی – **faarsee** (Farsi, Persian)

ف   **f**   بَرف – **barf** (snow)

ف   **f**   کَف – **kaf** (foam)

Practice writing what you heard in the audio several times and try to follow the steps.

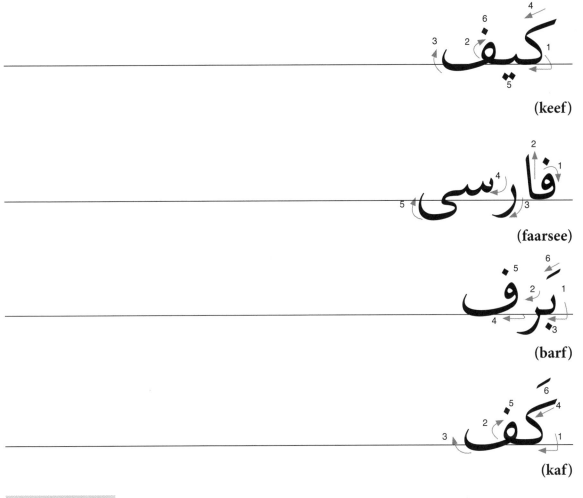

(keef)

(faarsee)

(barf)

(kaf)

Exercise 2.51 Listen to audio A02-51 and fill in the blanks.

۳. ـِـرشـــه   ۲. ـَـرـــند   ۱. ــارسـ ـــ

Exercise 2.52 Listen to audio A02-52 and fill in the blanks.

۲. ـیزیک   ۱. ـن

۴. ـوری   ۳. ـیلم

Exercise 2.53   Listen to audio A02-53 and transcribe it.

_____ ٢.   _____ ١.

_____ ٤.   _____ ٣.

 O

أ sounds like **o** in the English word *cone*. Like other short vowels (أ and إ), it takes an ا as a base for the ُ diacritic if the word starts with the sound أ. Like other diacritics, writing it is not mandatory and as you get more skilled in reading and writing, you will not need them.

cone

✎ Writing Rules

أ Initial does not attach. It is written standalone.
ُ Medial placed on all letters as a non-mandatory diacritic.

Look at the image below and follow the steps to write أ. Write it several times in the designated space.

(o)

Listen to audio A02-54 to familiarize yourself with the sound of اُ in several Farsi words.

اُ　　**o**　　اُردَک – **ordak** (duck)

ـُ　　**o**　　مُدیر – **modeer** (manager)

ـُ　　**p**　　مُشت – **mosht** (fist)

Practice writing what you heard in the audio several times and try to follow the steps.

(ordak)

(modeer)

(mosht)

Exercise 2.54　Complete the following.

١.　ش + ـُ + ت + ـُ + ر = _____

٢.　م + ـُ + د + ى + ر = _____

٣.　ت + ـُ + ن + د = _____

Exercise 2.55   Listen to audio A02-55 and fill in the blanks.

‎۳. ‫ید‬ ‫ــ ــ ــ‬   ‎۲. ‫ک ــ ر ــ‬   ‎۱. ‫ــ م‬

Exercise 2.56   Listen to audio A02-56 and transcribe it.

‎۲. _____   ‎۱. _____

‎۴. _____   ‎۳. _____

گ گ گ **Gaaf**
(g)

goose

گ sounds like **g** in the English word *goose*. As you heard in audio A02-01, its name is **gaaf** on the alphabet. گ has two initial/medial and final detached/attached forms.

 Writing Rules

گ   Initial/medial attaches on both sides.
گ   Final detached/attached attaches on the right to the letters that attach on the left.

Look at the image below and follow the steps to write گ. Write it several times in the designated space.

(g)

Listen to audio A02-57 to familiarize yourself with the sound of گ in several Farsi words.

گ   **g**   گُرگ   –   **gorg** (wolf)

گ   **g**   گربه   –   **gorbe** (cat)

گ   **g**   بَرگ   –   **barg** (leaf)

گ   **g**   نَهَنگ   –   **nahang** (whale)

Practice writing what you heard in the audio several times and try to follow the steps.

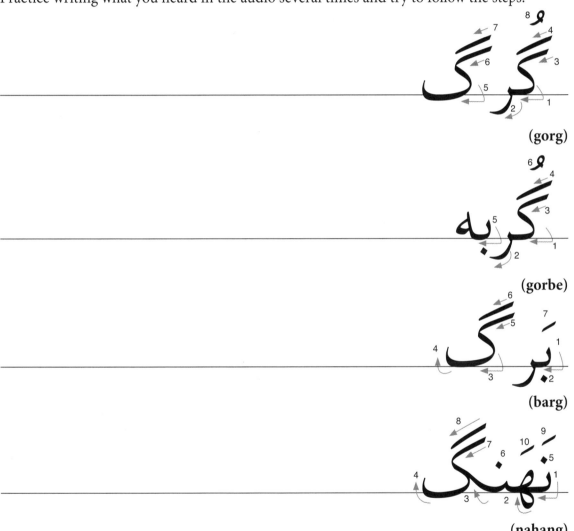

(gorg)

(gorbe)

(barg)

(nahang)

Exercise 2.57   Complete the following.

١.   ــــــــــــــــــ = ر + و + گ + ن + ـَ + ا   .١

٢.   ــــــــــــــــــ = گ + ـُ + ر + گ   .٢

٣.   ــــــــــــــــــ = ت + ش + و + گ   .٣

Exercise 2.58   Listen to audio A02-58 and fill in the blanks.

٢.   ـــ ن ـــ   ١.   ـــ وش

٤.   ـــ را ـــ   ٣.   ـــ سَن ـــ ي ـــ

Exercise 2.59   Listen to audio A02-59 and transcribe it.

٢.   ــــــــــــــــــ   ١.   ــــــــــــــــــ

٤.   ــــــــــــــــــ   ٣.   ــــــــــــــــــ

ق ـق Ghaaf (gh)

bonjour!

The sound for ق does not exist in English. It is pronounced from the back of the throat. Many native English speakers tend to confuse it with the گ (**g**) sound, but it sounds different. Listen to audio A02-60 to hear the ق (**gh**) sound and pay attention to its difference from گ (**g**). Note that the first word uses ق (**gh**) and the second one uses گ (**g**). You can see the two words have quite different definitions.

ق   بَرق – **bargh** (electricity)

گ   بَرگ – **barg** (leaf)

ق's name is **ghaaf** on the alphabet as you have heard in audio A02-01. It has two initial/medial and final detached/attached forms.

 Writing Rules

ق   Initial/medial attaches on both sides.

ق   Final detached/attached attaches on the right to the letters that attach on the left.

Look at the image below and follow the steps to write ق. Write it several times in the designated space.

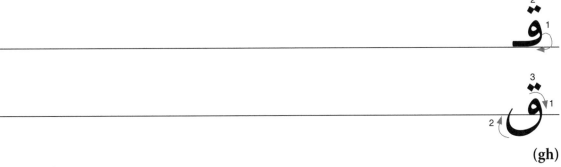

(gh)

 Writing Tip:

Like other letters with more than one dot, ق's dots can be written in the form of a straight line for ease of writing.

قَ   قَ

Listen to audio A02-61 to familiarize yourself with the sound of ق in several Farsi words.

ﻖ	**gh**	قوری –	**ghooree** (teapot)
ﻖ	**gh**	بُشقاب –	**boshghaab** (plate)
ق	**gh**	اُتاق –	**otaagh** (room)
ق	**gh**	بَرق –	**bargh** (electricity)

Practice writing what you heard in the audio several times and try to follow the steps.

(ghooree)

(boshghaab)

(otaagh)

(bargh)

Exercise 2.60   Complete the following.

١. ق + ر + ــَ + ش = ــــــــــــــــــــــــ

٢. ق + د + ــَ + ی + م + ی = ــــــــــــــــــــــــ

٣. ق + ــَ + ن + ا + ر + ی = ــــــــــــــــــــــــ

Exercise 2.61   Listen to audio A02-62 and fill in the blanks.

١. ــ ــ س   ٢. ــ ور ــ

٣. ــ ر ــ ــ

Exercise 2.62 Listen to audio A02-63 and transcribe it.

_____ .۲   _____ .۱

_____ .۴   _____ .۳

خ خـ **Khe**
(kh)

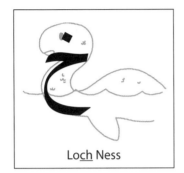

Loch Ness

خ is another sound that does not exist in English. It sounds like the *ch* in the Scottish body of water *Loch Ness*. The خ sound is a bit similar to *h* but with squeezed throat. Note that the *h* and the *kh* sound completely different in Farsi. خ is called **khe** in the alphabet as you heard in the audio A02-01.

Listen to audio A02-64 to listen to the خ (**kh**) sound and its comparison with *h*.

ه **h**   هاله – **haale** (halo)

خ **kh**   خاله – **khaale** (maternal aunt)

خ has two forms of initial/medial and final detached/attached.

 Writing Rules

خـ Initial/medial attaches on both sides.

خ Final detached/attached attaches on the right to the letters that attach on the left.

Look at the image below and follow the steps to write خ. Write it several times in the designated space.

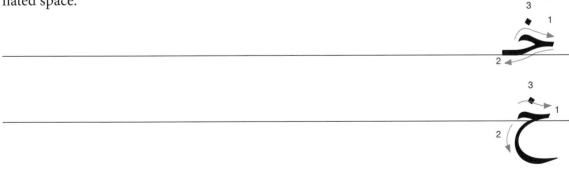

(kh)

Listen to the audio A02-65 to get familiar with the sound of خ in several Farsi words.

خـ **kh**   خاک – **khaak** (soil)

خـ **kh**   دِرَخت – **derakht** (tree)

خ   **kh**   یَخ – **yakh** (ice)

خ   **kh**   کاخ – **kaakh** (palace)

Practice writing the following what you heard in the audio several times and try to follow the steps.

(khaak)

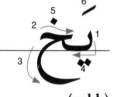

(derakht)

(yakh)

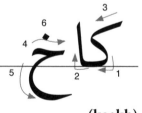

(kaakh)

Exercise 2.63   Complete the following.

١. خ + ا + ر = _____

٢. خ + َ + ر + ا + ب = _____

٣. ى + َ + خ = _____

Exercise 2.64   Listen to audio A02-66 and fill in the blanks.

٢. ____ ا ____ سو ____

١. ش ____ رگ ____

۴. ر ____ ____ دُ

٣. ____ و ____

Exercise 2.65   Listen to audio A02-67 and transcribe it.

٢. _____

١. _____

۴. _____

٣. _____

چ جـ **Che**
(ch)

chick

ج sounds like **ch** in the English word *chick*. Its name is **che** in the alphabet as you heard in audio A02-01. ج has two forms of initial/medial and final detached/attached.

Writing Rules

ﭼ   Initial/medial attaches on both sides.

ﺢ   Final detached/attached attaches on the right to the letters that attach on the left.

Look at the image below and follow the steps to write ﺢ. Write it several times in the designated space.

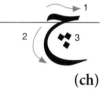

(ch)

 Writing Tip:

You can use an open circle instead of the three dots to simplify writing.

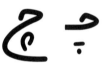

Listen to audio A02-68 to get familiar with the sound of ﺢ in several Farsi words.

ﭼ	ch	چرا	–	**cheraa** (why)
ﭼ	ch	چَهار	–	**chaahaar** (four)
ﺞ	ch	پارچ	–	**paarch** (pitcher)
ﺞ	ch	قارچ	–	**ghaarch** (mushroom)

Practice writing the following what you heard in the audio several times and try to follow the steps.

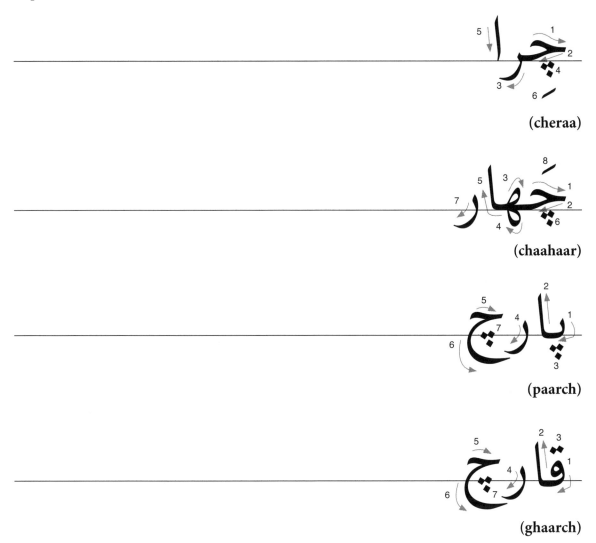

(cheraa)

(chaahaar)

(paarch)

(ghaarch)

Exercise 2.66   Complete the following.

١ . پ + ا + ر + چ + ه = ــــــــــــــ

٢ . چ + ــَـ + ر + ا = ــــــــــــــ

٣ . چ + ــَـ + ا + ر + ش + ــَـ + ن + ب + ه = ــــــــــــــ

Exercise 2.67   Listen to audio A02-69 and fill in the blanks.

٣ . ای___   ٢ . ___ش____   ١ . و___ا___

Exercise 2.68   Listen to audio A02-70 and transcribe it.

٢ . _____   ١ . _____

٤ . _____   ٣ . _____

ه ﻪ ﻬ ﻫ **He**
(h)

happy

ه sounds like **h** in the English word *happy*. Its name is **he** in the alphabet as you have heard in audio A02-01. ه has four forms of initial, medial, final attached, and final detached.

✎ Writing Rules

ﻫ   Initial attaches on the right.

ﻬ   Medial attaches on both sides.

ﻪ   Final attached attaches on the right.

ه   Final detached is written standalone.

Look at the image below and follow the steps to write ه. Write it several times in the designated space. Note that the medial and initial forms have several variations in printing and handwriting that might look different from what what is shown here.

(h)

Listen to audio A02-71 to get familiar with the sound of ه in several Farsi words.

ـه	h	هَمه –	**hame** (all)
ـهـ	h	تِهران –	**tehraan** (Tehran, the capital of Iran)
ـه	h	مِه –	**meh** (fog)
ه	h	ماه –	**maah** (moon)

Practice writing the following what you heard in the audio several times and try to follow the steps.

(hame)

(tehraan)

(meh)

(maah)

Exercise 2.69 Complete the following.

١. د + ا + ن + ــ + ش + گ + ا + ه = ــــــــــــ

٢. س + ی + ا + ه = ــــــــــــــــــــ

٣. ه + ــَ + و + ی + ج = ــــــــــــــــــــ

Exercise 2.70 Listen to audio A02-72 and fill in the blanks.

٢. ما ـــ ـــ   ١. ـــمیشـــ

                              ٣. با ـــوش

Exercise 2.71 Listen to audio A02-73 and transcribe it.

٢. ــــــــــــ   ١. ــــــــــــ

٤. ــــــــــــ   ٣. ــــــــــــ

ج ـجـ **Jeem**
(j)

jar

ج sounds like **j** in the English word *jar*. It is called **jeem** in the alphabet as you have heard in audio A02-01. It has two forms of initial/medial and final detached/attached.

✎ Writing Rules

ج   Initial/medial attaches on both sides.

ج   Final attached/detached attaches on the right to the letters that attach on the left.

Look at the image below and follow the steps to write ج. Write it several times in the designated space.

(j)

Listen to audio A02-74 to get familiar with the sound of ج in several Farsi words.

جـ j جوراب – **jooraab** (sock)

جـ j جوجه – **jooje** (chick)

ج j برنج – **berenj** (rice)

ج j تاج – **taaj** (crown)

Practice what you heard in the audio several times and try to follow the steps.

(joorab)

(jooje)

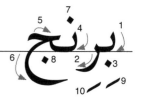

(berenj)

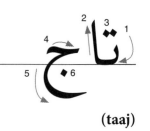

(taaj)

Exercise 2.72   Complete the following.

١.   پ + ‍َ + ن + ج = _____

٢.   ک + ا + ج = _____

٣.   ج + ‍َ + و + ا + ن = _____

Exercise 2.73   Listen to audio A02-75 and fill in the blanks.

٢.   ___ ن___ره   ١.   ___ ___ ن___ ___

۴.   مَس‍ ___ ___   ٣.   ___شن

Exercise 2.74   Listen to audio A02-76 and transcribe it.

٢.   _____   ١.   _____

۴.   _____   ٣.   _____

ل ل **Laam**
(l)

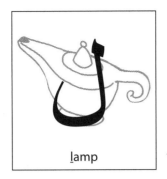

lamp

ل sounds like **l** in the English word *lamp*. It is called **laam** in the alphabet as you heard in audio A02-01. ل has two forms of initial/medial and final attached/detached.

 Writing Rules

ل   Initial/medial attaches on both sides.

ل   Final attached/detached attaches on the right.

Look at the image below and follow the steps to write ل. Write it several times in the designated space.

(l)

Listen to audio A02-77 to get familiar with the sound of ل in several Farsi words.

ل   l   لِباس – **lebaas** (clothing)

ل   l   گیلاس – **geelaas** (cherry)

ل   l   پول – **pool** (money)

ل   l   سال – **saal** (year)

Practice writing the following what you heard in the audio several times and follow the steps.

(lebaas)

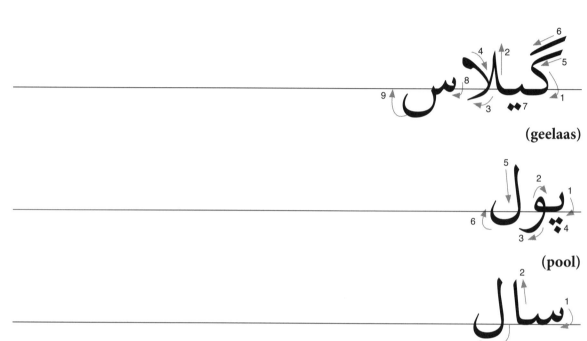

(geelaas)

(pool)

(saal)

Exercise 2.75   Complete the following.

‫۱.   پ + و + ل = _____‬

‫۲.   ل + ‫ـِ‬ + ی + ل + ا = _____‬

‫۳.   ل + و + ل + ٥ = _____‬

Exercise 2.76   Listen to audio A02-78 and fill in the blanks.

٣. ــــــيوا ــــــ   ٢. ــــــ ــــــ سَــــم   ١. گُ ــــــ

Exercise 2.77   Listen to audio A02-79 and transcribe it.

٢. _____   ١. _____

٤. _____   ٣. _____

violin

و **Vaav**
(v)

و looks similar to the long vowel او (**oo**) covered before, but it sounds like **v** in the English word *violin*, not *oo*. Unlike او (**oo**), و (**v**) has only one form. و (**v**) is called **vaav** on the alphabet as you heard in audio A02-01.

 Writing Rules

و   Initial/medial/final attaches on the right.

 Reading Tip:

There are a couple of ways to distinguish between و and او but they cannot be applied to all words.
1. Being a long vowel, او (**oo**) does not get a diacritic, but و (**v**) gets them as it is a consonant.
2. و (**v**) has only one form, so if the word starts with a و (**v**), it is read as **v** and not **oo**.

Having said that, practice and exposure to the language is the best way of reading and writing correctly as diacritics are rarely used.

Look at the image below and follow the steps to write و. Write it several times in the designated space.

_____

Listen to audio A02-80 to get familiar with the sound of و in several Farsi words.

و   v   وَزن – **vazn** (weight)

و   v   آواز – **aavaaz** (song)

و   v   وَرزِش – **varzesh** (exercise)

Practice what you heard in the audio several times and try to follow the steps.

_____

(vazn)

_____

(aavaaz)

_____

(varzesh)

Exercise 2.78 Complete the following.

١. د + ـَ + و + ـَ + ن + د + ه = _____

٢. ک + ـِ + ش + ا + و + ـَ + ر + ز = _____

٣. د + ا + و + ـَ + ر = _____

Exercise 2.79 Listen to audio A02-81 and fill in the blanks.

١. دَ __ __ د   ٢. __ زشکا __   ٣. پَ __ __ از

Exercise 2.80 Listen to audio A02-82 and transcribe it.

٣. _____   ٢. _____   ١. _____

خوا Khaa   خوا is considered an exception in reading and writing. It looks as if it should be read as **khavaa**, but its correct pronunciation is **khaa**. There are not many words that use this form and there are a few exceptions to it, which is beyond the scope of this book.

Writing Rules

خوا attaches on the right.

Look at the image below and follow the steps to write خوا. Write it several times in the desig-nated space.

(khaa)

Listen to audio A02-83 to get familiar with the sound of خوا in several Farsi words.

خوا **khaa**   خواهَر – **khaahar** (sister)

خوا **khaa**   خواهِش – **khaahesh** (request)

خوا **khaa**   خواب – **khaab** (sleep)

Practice writing the following what you heard in the audio several times and try to follow the steps.

(khaahar)

(khaahesh)

(khaab)

Exercise 2.81   Complete the following.

۱. گ + ی + ا + ه + خ + و + ا + ر = _____

۲. خ + و + ا + ب + ی + د + ﹷ + ن = _____

۳. خ + و + ا + ن + ﹷ + ن + د + ه = _____

Exercise 2.82   Listen to audio A02-84 and fill in the blanks.

۳. خـ__اندَ__   ۲. __و__نـ__ __   ۱. خو__ هِش

Exercise 2.83   Listen to audio A02-85 and transcribe it.

۳. _____   ۲. _____   ۱. _____

ژ **Zhe**
(zh)

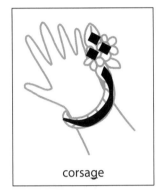

corsage

The ژ sounds like the second **g** in the word *corsage*. ژ is called **zhe** in the Farsi alphabet as you heard in audio A02-01. It has only one form and follows the same rules as ر and ز.

✎ Writing Rules

ژ   Initial/medial/final attaches on the right.

✍ Writing Tip:

ژ is another letter with three dots, so you can replace the dots with an open circle.

ژ

Look at the image below and follow the steps to write ژ. Write it several times in the desig-nated space.

(zh)

Listen to audio A02-86 to get familiar with the sound of ژ in several Farsi words.

ژ   **zh**   ژاکِت – **zhaaket** (cardigan)

ژ   **zh**   ژاپُن – **zhaapon** (Japan)

ژ   **zh**   ژاله – **zhaale** (a feminine name)

Practice writing what you heard in the audio several times and try to follow the steps.

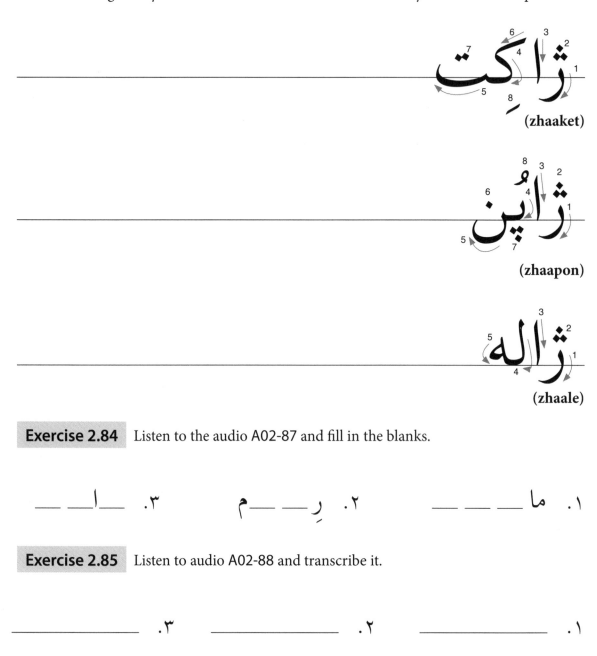

ژاکت
(zhaaket)

ژاپُن
(zhaapon)

ژاله
(zhaale)

Exercise 2.84   Listen to the audio A02-87 and fill in the blanks.

۳. ــ ــاــ   ۲. رِــ ــم   ۱. ما ــ ــ ــ ــ

Exercise 2.85   Listen to audio A02-88 and transcribe it.

۳. _____   ۲. _____   ۱. _____

ص ـصـ ص **Saad**
(s)

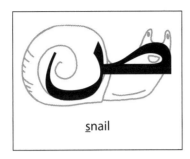

snail

ص sounds like **s** in the English word *snail*. You have already learned another letter that sounds identical: س (**s**). ص is called **saad** on the alphabet as you heard in audio A02-01.

 Writing Tip:

As you learn the new words, try to memorize the type of **s** letter they use. ص (**s**) has two forms of initial/medial and final attached/detached.

 Writing Rules

ـصـ   Initial/medial attaches on both sides.

ص   Final attached/detached attaches on the right.

Look at the image below and follow the steps to write ص.

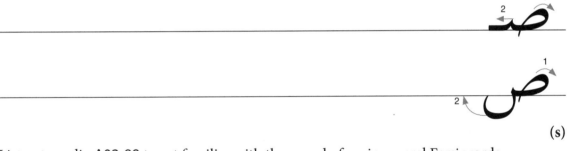

(s)

Listen to audio A02-89 to get familiar with the sound of ص in several Farsi words.

ـصـ	**s**	صابون –	**saaboon** (soap)
ـصـ	**s**	صِدا –	**sedaa** (sound, voice)
ص	**s**	مَخصوص –	**makhsoos** (special)

Practice writing what you heard in the audio several times and try to follow the steps. Try to memorize the type of s letter as well.

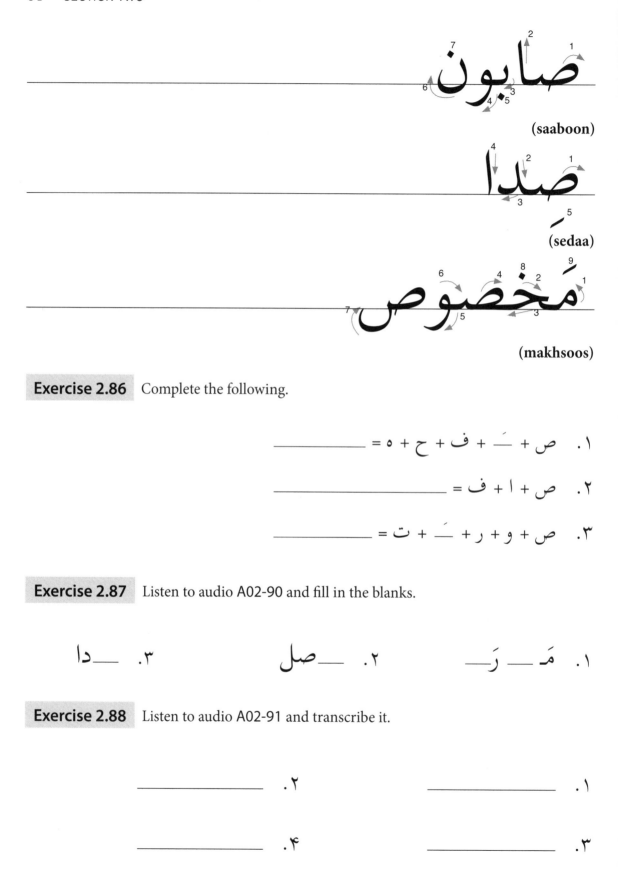

صابون
(saaboon)

صَدا
(sedaa)

مُخْصوص
(makhsoos)

Exercise 2.86   Complete the following.

١.   ص + ـَ + ف + ح + ه = ــــــــــــــ

٢.   ص + ا + ف = ــــــــــــــ

٣.   ص + و + ر + ـَ + ت = ــــــــــــــ

Exercise 2.87   Listen to audio A02-90 and fill in the blanks.

١. مَ ــ رَ ــ   ٢. ــ صل   ٣. ــ دا

Exercise 2.88   Listen to audio A02-91 and transcribe it.

٢. ــــــــــــــ   ١. ــــــــــــــ

٤. ــــــــــــــ   ٣. ــــــــــــــ

ح ‹ حـ › **He**
(h)

<u>h</u>eart

ح sounds like **h** in the English word *heart*. ح is called **he** in the alphabet as you heard in the audio A02-01. You have already learned another letter that sounds like *h* and identical to ح: it is ه. Try to pay attention to the type of **h** letter as you learn more. ح has two forms of initial/medial and final attached/detached.

 ## Writing Rules

حـ   Initial/medial attaches on both sides.
ح   Final attached/detached attaches on the right.

Look at the image below and follow the steps to write ح.

(h)

Listen to audio A02-92 to get familiar with the sound of ح in several Farsi words.

حـ   **h**   حیوان   – **heyvaan** (animal)
حـ   **h**   حَرکَت   – **harekat** (movement)
ح   **h**   صُبح   – **sobh** (morning)

Practice writing the following what you heard in the audio several times and try to follow the steps. Try to memorize the type of *h* letter as well.

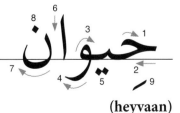

(heyvaan)

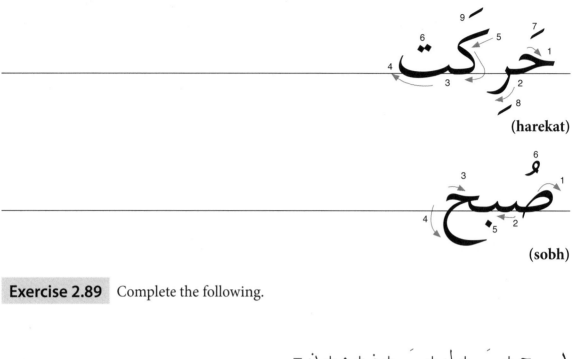

(harekat)

(sobh)

Exercise 2.89   Complete the following.

١. ح + ﹷ + ل + ﹷ + ز + و + ن = _____

٢. خ + و + ش + ح + ا + ل = _____

Exercise 2.90   Listen to audio A02-93 and fill in the blanks.

١. تَفـ ___ ريـ ___   ٢. ___ رار ___   ٣. سا ___ ___

Exercise 2.91   Listen to audio A02-94 and transcribe it.

١. _____   ٢. _____   ٣. _____

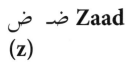

ض ضـ **Zaad**
(z)

zoo

ض sounds like **z** in the English word *zebra*. You have already learned ز that sounds the same as ض. Try to memorize the type of *z* letter the words use. ض is called **zaad** on the alphabet as you heard in audio A02-01. It has two forms of initial/medial and final attached/detached.

✎ **Writing Rules**

ضـ Initial/medial attaches on both sides.

ض Final attached detached attaches on the right.

Look at the image below and follow the steps to write ض.

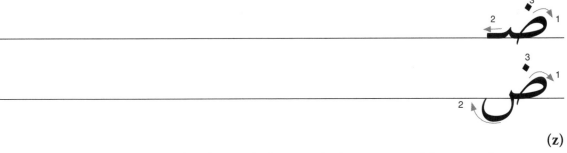

(z)

Listen to audio A02-95 to get familiar with the sound of ض in several Farsi words.

ضـ   z   ریاضی   – **reeyaazee** (math)

ضـ   z   قاضی   – **ghaazee** (judge)

ض   z   مَریض   – **mareez** (patient, sick)

Practice writing the following what you heard in the audio several times and try to follow the steps. Try to memorize the type of *z* letter as well.

(reeyaazee)

(ghaazee)

(mareez)

Exercise 2.92   Listen to audio A02-96 and fill in the blanks.

٣. حا___ر   ٢. ___رب___   ١. فَ___ ___

Exercise 2.93   Listen to audio A02-97 and transcribe it.

٣. _____   ٢. _____   ١. _____

ط **Taa**
(t)

ṭulip

ط sounds like **t** in the English word *tulip*. You have already learned another **t** sounding letter: ت. ط has only one form. ط is called **taa** in the alphabet as you heard in the audio A02-01.

 Writing Tip:

As you learn new letters and words, pay attention to the type of *t* the words use.

 Writing Rules

ط   Initial/medial/final attaches on both sides.

Look at the image below and follow the steps to write ط.

(t)

Listen to audio A02-98 to get familiar with the sound of ط in several Farsi words.

ط t طوطی – **tootee** (parrot)
ط t حَیاط – **hayaat** (yard)
ط t طلا – **talaa** (gold)

Practice writing the following what you heard in the audio several times and try to follow the steps. Try to memorize the type of **t** letter as well.

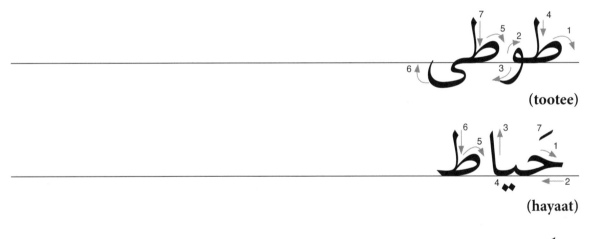

(tootee)

(hayaat)

(talaa)

Exercise 2.94   Listen to audio A02-99 and fill in the blanks.

ر— — . ۱   — — سَـ . ۲   —ل— . ۳

Exercise 2.95   Listen to audio A02-100 and transcribe it.

_____ .٣   _____ .٢   _____ .١

ظ **Zaa**
(z)

zucchini

ظ sounds like **z** in the English word *zucchini*. You have already learned two more *z* sounding letters: ض and ظ ز. is called **zaa** in the alphabet as you heard in the audio A02-01. ظ has only one form.

    Writing Tip:

Pay attention to the type of *z* used in the new words.

 Writing Rules

ظ   Initial/medial/final attaches on both sides.

Look at the image below and follow the steps to write ظ.

ظ

(z)

Listen to audio A02-101 to get familiar with the sound of ظ in several Farsi words.

ظ   z   ظُهر – **zohr** (noon)
ظ   z   ظَرف – **zarf** (dish)

Practice writing what you heard in the audio several times and try to follow the steps. Try to memorize the type of t letter as well.

(zohr)

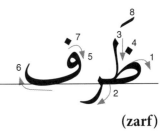

(**zarf**)

Exercise 2.96   Listen to audio A02-102 and fill in the blanks.

۲ . مُوا ___ ___   ۱ . خُدا ___ ا ___ ___

Exercise 2.97   Listen to audio A02-103 and transcribe it.

۳ . _____   ۲ . _____   ۱ . _____

ع ع ع ع **Ein**

Sea of Oman

The ع sound is another nonexistent sound in English. It is called **ein** in the alphabet as you heard in the audio A02-01.

ع has four forms of initial, medial, final attached, and final detached. In general, ع is like a consonant ا and is often accompanied by the vowels before or after it. Its sound is like ا, but you suddenly stop, then continue the pronunciation, like a short pause.

Listen to audio A02-104 to familiarize yourself with the sound of ع. The pause that you hear is the **ein** pronunciation.

مَعبَد **ein** – **ma'bad** (temple)

✎ Writing Rules

ع   Initial attaches on the left.
ع   Medial attaches on both sides.

ع   Final attached attaches on the right.
ع   Final detached is standalone.

Look at the image below and follow the steps to write ع.

(ein)

Listen to audio A02-105 to familiarize yourself with the sound of ع in several Farsi words. Pay attention to how they sound when they accompany vowels compared to when they do not.

عـ   عَلی – **alee** (Ali, a masculine name)

ـعـ   بَعد – **ba'd** (then)

عـ   باعِث – **baa'es** (cause)

ع   شُروع – **shoroo'** (begin)

Exercise 2.98   Complete the following.

١. م + ـَ + ع + ب + ـَ + د = _____

٢. د + ـُ + ع + ا = _____

٣. س + ـَ + ع + ی + د = _____

Writing Tip:

Note that sometimes ع sounds just like ا, especially when it is in the beginning of the word. So, try to pay attention to the spellings as you learn.

Practice writing what you heard in the audio several times and try to follow the steps.

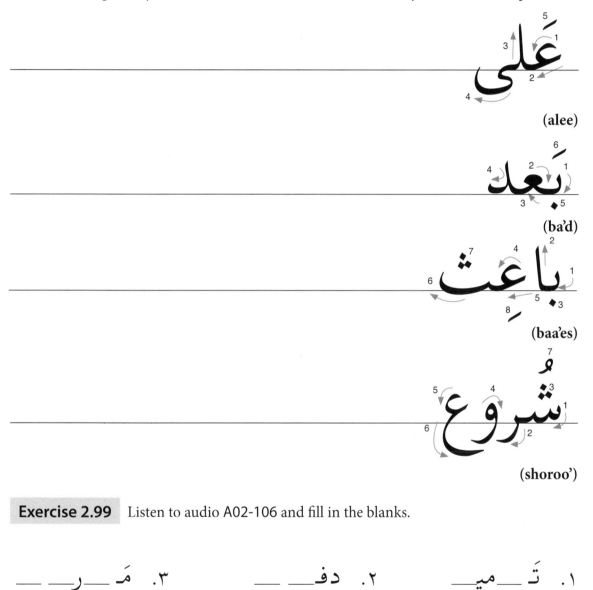

(alee)

(ba'd)

(baa'es)

(shoroo')

Exercise 2.99 Listen to audio A02-106 and fill in the blanks.

۱. تَ__میـ__ ۲. دِ__ف__ __ ۳. مَ__ر__ __ __

Exercise 2.100   Listen to audio A02-107 and transcribe it.

_____ ٣.   _____ ٢.   _____ ١.

غ ـغ ـغـ غـ **Ghein**
(gh)

"Augh! My backpack
is too heavy!"

غ is another sound that does not exist in English. It sounds identical to ق (**gh**), only looks different. غ is called **ghein** in the alphabet as you heard in the audio A02-01. It has four forms of initial, medial, final attached, and final detached.

 Writing Rules

غـ   Attaches on the left.

ـغـ   Attaches on both sides.

ـغ   Attaches on the left.

غ   Does not attach, written standalone.

Look at the image below and follow the steps to write غ.

(gh)

 Writing Tip:

As you learn the letters try to remember what **gh** sounds they use.

Listen to audio A02-108 to get familiar with the sound of غ in several Farsi words.

غ	**gh**	غُنچه –	**ghonche** (flower bud)
ـغـ	**gh**	جُغد –	**joghd** (owl)
ـغ	**gh**	جیغ –	**jeegh** (scream)
غ	**gh**	مُرغ –	**morgh** (chicken)

Practice writing what you heard in the audio several times and try to follow the steps.

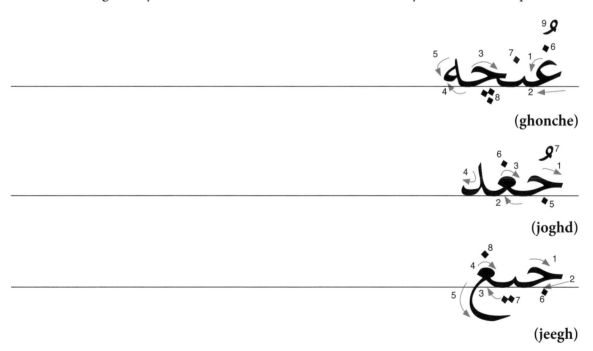

(ghonche)

(joghd)

(jeegh)

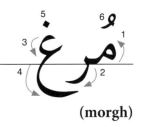

(morgh)

Exercise 2.101 Complete the following.

١. ب + ا + غ + ب + ا + ن = _____

٢. د + ﹷ + م + ا + غ = _____

Exercise 2.102 Listen to audio A02-109 and fill in the blanks.

٢. ت __ __ __   ١. با__

Exercise 2.103 Listen to audio A02-110 and transcribe it.

٣. _____   ٢. _____   ١. _____

ث ثـ ث **Se**
(s)

safe

ث is another **s** sound, sounding identical to the other **s** sound covered earlier in this section. They were: س and ص. It only looks different and is less frequently used. ث is called **se** in the alphabet as you heard in the audio A02-01. It has two forms of initial/medial and final attached/detached.

✎ **Writing Rules**
ثـ   Initial/medial attaches on both sides.
ث   Final attached/detached attaches on the right.

Look at the image below and follow the steps to write ث.

(s)

Listen to audio A02-111 to familiarize yourself with the sound of ث in several Farsi words.

ث s كَثيف – **kaseef** (dirty, messy)

ث s ثروَتمَند – **servatmand** (wealthy)

ث s أثاث – **asaas** (furnishings, the stuff in a home)

Practice writing the following what you heard on the audio several times and try to follow the steps. Just like other multi-dot letters, you can use an open circle instead of the three dots to simplify writing.

(kaseef)

(servatmand)

(asaas)

Exercise 2.104   Complete the following.

١ .   ث + ا + ن + ى + ه = _____

٢ .   م + ـِ + ث + ا + ل = _____

Exercise 2.105   Listen to audio A02-112 and fill in the blanks.

٢ .   أَ__ __ ___   ١ .   لَ__ __ ___

Exercise 2.106   Listen to audio A02-113 and transcribe it.

٢ .   _____   ١ .   _____

ذ **Zaal**
(z)

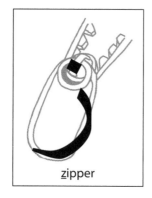

zipper

ذ is another **z** sounding letter, which sounds identical to ز, ظ, and ض. It is rather less frequently used than the others. ذ has only one form and it is called **zaal** on the alphabet as you heard in the audio A02-01.

 Writing Rules

ذ   Initial/medial/ final attaches on the right.

Look at the image below and follow the steps to write ذ.

(z)

Listen to audio A02-114 to get familiar with the sound of ذ in several Farsi words.

ذ   z   غَذا – **ghazaa** (food)

ذ   z   لَذیذ – **lazeez** (tasty)

Practice writing what you heard in the audio several times and try to follow the steps.

(ghazaa)

(lazeez)

Exercise 2.107 Listen to audio A02-115 and fill in the blanks.

Exercise 2.108 Listen to audio A02-116 and transcribe it.

_____ ۱.

ﹽ Tashdeed

A giraffe has two hard horns (called ossicones).
A **tashdeed** means two hard sounds.

ﹽ is not a letter, but a diacritic. Unlike most other diacritics, writing this one is required. The meaning of the word **tashdeed** is intensification. It means when it is placed on top of the letter, you read that letter with stress. For example in the word لذَّت, you see that ﹽ is placed on top of ذ. It means you pronounce ذ stronger than other letters. Basically ﹽ multiplies the letter as shown below:

$$لذَّت = لذ + ذَت$$

As you can see, the ذ is doubled by the **tashdeed**, the first one with no vowel, the second one read with the diacritic on it. For pronunciation purposes the **tashdeed** is shown by doubling the letter in the Romanized words.

(z)

Listen to audio A02-117 to get familiar with the pronunciation of ﹽ in several words.

لذَّت	لذ ذَت –	**lezzat** (joy)
اَوَّل	اَو وَل –	**avval** (first)
بَچّه	بَچ چه –	**bachche** (child, kid)
مُرَبّا	مُرَب با –	**morabbaa** (jam, fruit jelly)

Now practice writing what you heard in the audio several times and try to follow the steps.

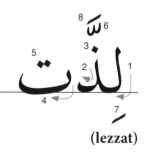

(lezzat)

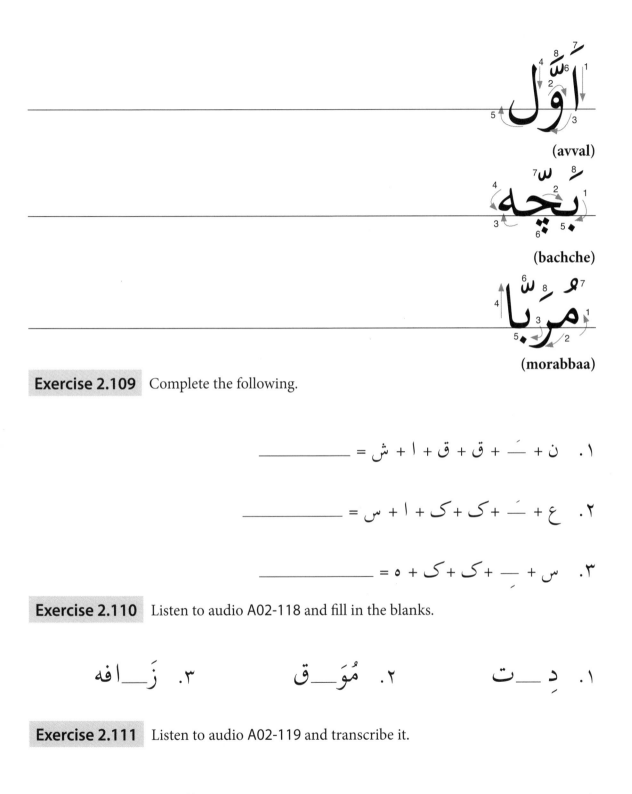

اَوَّل

(avval)

بچه

(bachche)

مُرَبّا

(morabbaa)

Exercise 2.109 Complete the following.

١.   ن + ـَ + ق + ق + ا + ش = _____

٢.   ع + ـَ + ک + ک + ا + س = _____

٣.   س + ـِ + ک + ک + ه = _____

Exercise 2.110 Listen to audio A02-118 and fill in the blanks.

١. دِ___ت   ٢. مُوَ___ق   ٣. زَ___افه

Exercise 2.111 Listen to audio A02-119 and transcribe it.

٢. _____   ١. _____

ء أ ؤ ئ ئ **Hamze**   ء is another sound that has no equivalent in English. It sounds the same as ع, only looks different. **Hamze** is the small diacritic you see on top of the vowels that looks similar to the number 6 in Farsi. **Hamze** is only placed on long vowels, or used alone at the end of the word. It has many forms, but the main ones are medial and final. **Hamze** has no initial form because in the beginning of the word it just becomes ا. There are some rules as to what long vowel becomes the base of the **hamze**, which is out of the scope of this book. You only need to memorize what words use **hamze**, how they are spelled, and the fact that it sounds like an **ein**, as there are not many words with **hamze**. Also, recently ء is being replaced by ی, but since the change has not been very consistent, ء is still used sometimes.

✎ Writing Rules

ؤ، ئ   The medial form is either a و or a dotless ی with a **hamze** on top of it and depending on the letter used they follow the و or the ی rules.

ئ، إ، أ   Final attached/detached attaches on the right.

ء   The final form does not attach and is used standalone.

Look at the image below and follow the steps to write ء.

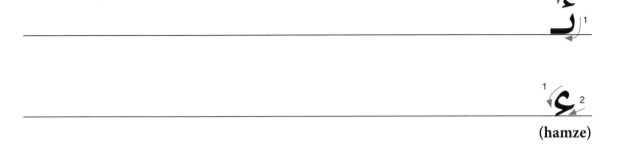

(hamze)

Listen to audio A02-120 to get familiar with the sound of ء in several Farsi words.

منشأ – **mansha'** (source)

سوء – **soo'** (bad)

مسئول – **mas'ool** (responsible)

Practice writing the following what you heard in the audio several times and try to follow the steps.

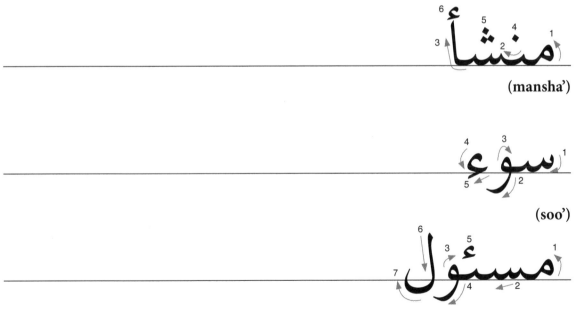

(mansha')

(soo')

(mas'ool)

Exercise 2.112   Complete the following.

$$ \underline{\hspace{4cm}} = \text{ت} + \underset{\cdot}{\text{\_}} + \text{ی} + \text{ل} + \text{و} + \text{ئ} + \text{س} + \underset{\cdot}{\text{\_}} + \text{م} \quad .\text{۱} $$

$$ \underline{\hspace{4cm}} = \text{ء} + \text{و} + \text{س} \quad .\text{۲} $$

Exercise 2.113   Listen to audio A02-121 and transcribe it.

$$ \underline{\hspace{4cm}} \quad .\text{۲} \qquad\qquad \underline{\hspace{4cm}} \quad .\text{۱} $$

اً Tanveen

man

Tanveen is a diacritic with Arabic origin. Usually, it is added to the end of adjectives and creates adverbs. Note that we cannot create new adverbs with **tanveen**. We can only use the existing ones in Farsi.

There are several types of **tanveen** in Arabic, but only one of them is used in Farsi. **Tanveen** sounds like **an**. It has only one final form.

✎ Writing Rules

اً   Final attached/detached attaches on the right.

Now look at the image below and practice writing **tanveen**.

(tanveen)

Listen to audio A02-122 to get familiar with several adverbs using **tanveen**.

واقِعاً – **vaaghe'an** (really)

دائماً – **daa'eman** (constantly)

بَعداً – **ba'dan** (later)

Practice writing the following what you heard in the audio several times and try to follow the steps.

وَاقِعاً

(vaaghe'an)

دائماً

(daa'eman)

بَعداً

(ba'dan)

Recently, some prefer to replace the traditional **tanveen** with how it actually sounds. So instead of writing اً, they write ـَن. For example, واقعاً becomes واقِعَن and بعداً becomes بَعدَن. This is another variation of **tanveen** and can be used on all words that use **tanveen**.

Exercise 2.114 Listen to audio A02-123 and transcribe it.

_____ ۲.   _____ ۱.

_____ ۴.   _____ ۳.

Persian Numbers 10 and Larger

In the previous section you learned numbers 0 to 10 as well as writing numbers in digit form. In this section, you will learn how to read and write numbers 10 and larger.

Numbers 11-19

11 to 19 have the suffix *dah* at the end. As you know دَه (**dah**) in Farsi means 10. So the numbers with a *dah* at the end are the 11–19.

Listen to audio A02-124 to get familiar with numbers 11-19.

١١ (eleven) **yaazdah**

١٢ (twelve) **davaazdah**

١٣ (thirteen) **seezdah**

١۴ (fourteen) **chaahaardah**

١۵ (fifteen) **paanzdah**

١۶ (sixteen) **shaanzdah**

١٧ (seventeen) **hefdah**

١٨ (eighteen) **hejdah**

١٩ (nineteen) **noozdah**

Exercise 2.115   Listen to audio A02-125 and transcribe the numbers in Farsi digits.

٣. _____   ٢. _____   ١. _____

٥. _____   ۴. _____

Numbers 20-100

In order to read and write numbers 20 to 100, you need to know the tens first.
Listen to audio A02-126 to get familiar with the 20–100.

٢٠   بیست (twenty) **beest**

٣٠   سی (thirty) **see**

۴٠   چِهِل (forty) **chehel**

۵٠   پَنجاه (fifty) **panjaah**

۶٠   شَصت (sixty) **shast**

٧٠   هَفتاد (seventy) **haftaad**

٨٠   هَشتاد (eighty) **hashtaad**

٩٠   نَوَد (ninety) **navad**

١٠٠   صَد (one hundred) **sad**

Exercise 2.116 Listen to audio A02-127 and transcribe it in Farsi digits.

۱) _____   ۲) _____   ۳) _____

۴) _____   ۵) _____   ۶) _____

۷) _____   ۸) _____

Now for the two digit numbers with ones, follow the following rule:

Tens + o + Ones

For example, ۲۱ is یک + o + بیست (**beest-o-yek**), or ۳۵ is پَنج + o + سی.
The "o" part is a variation of وَ (**va**) which means *and* in Farsi. It is very common to use **o** instead of **va**. In Numbers however, we only use o. So the two digits are tens + and + ones.

Exercise 2.117 Listen to audio A02-128 and fill in the blanks.

۱) ۲__   ۲) __ ۵   ۳) __ ۶

۴) __ ۸   ۵) __ __   ۶) ۸ __

۷) __ ۳   ۸) __ __

Exercise 2.118 Listen to audio A02-129 and transcribe it in Farsi digits.

۱) _____   ۲) _____   ۳) _____

۴) _____   ۵) _____   ۶) _____

۷) _____   ۸) _____

Numbers 100-1,000

For numbers 100 to 1,000, you need to know the hundreds, and then follow the same rule of the two digits, only adding hundreds to it.

Listen to the audio A02-130 to get familiar with the Farsi hundreds.

١٠٠	(100) **sad**	۶٠٠	(600) **sheshsad**
٢٠٠	(200) **deveest**	٧٠٠	(700) **haftsad**
٣٠٠	(300) **seesad**	٨٠٠	(800) **hashtsad**
۴٠٠	(400) **chahaarsad**	٩٠٠	(900) **nohsad**
۵٠٠	(500) **paansad**	١٠٠٠	(1,000) **hezaar**

Exercise 2.119   Listen to audio A02-131 and transcribe it in Farsi digits.

١) —————   ٢) —————   ٣) —————

۴) —————   ۵) —————   ۶) —————

Three-Digit Numbers Rule

Follow this rule in the three-digit numbers:
Hundreds + o + Tens + o + Ones

For example, for the number ٢۴٣, you say ٣٠٠ o ۴٠ o ٢ (**seesad o chehel o do**).

Exercise 2.120   Listen to audio A02-132 and transcribe it in Farsi digits.

١) —————   ٢) —————   ٣) —————

۴) —————   ۵) —————   ۶) —————

٧) —————   ٨) —————

Numbers over 1,000

For numbers over one thousand, you follow the same rule, only add the thousands, millions, billions, etc. Only mention how many thousands, millions, etc. are in the number. So 2,000 is simply the number 2 and the word "thousand," which is **do hezaar**. Or 8,000 is the number 8 and the word for thousand, **hasht hezaar**.

Listen to audio A02-133 to get familiar with larger numbers.

هِزار – **hezaar** (thousand)   میلیارد – **melyaard** (billion)

میلیون – **melyoon** (million)

Billions + o + millions + o + thousands + o + hundreds + o + tens + o + ones

Example

۲,۳۷۶,۰۹۸

2 melyoon o seesad o haftaad o shesh hezaar o navad o hasht

Exercise 2.121   Listen to audio A02-134 and transcribe it in Farsi numbers.

۱) ——————————   ۲) ——————————

۳) ——————————   ۴) ——————————

۵) ——————————   ۶) ——————————

۷) ——————————   ۸) ——————————

Reading and Writing Practice

In this section you learn topic-specific vocabulary and practice reading and writing. Below you will find numbered lists of the countries of the world in Farsi. The numbers correspond to the numbers on the maps. You do not have to learn the names of all the countries to learn Farsi. This section serves more as a listening/reading practice to familiarize yourself with Farsi sounds as well as a reference.

The Middle East (Iran and Its Neighbors)

Below is a list of the countries of the Middle East. Listen to audio A03-01 and learn the names of Iran's neighbors.

1. عَراق (**araagh**: Iraq)
2. تُرکیه (**torkeeye**: Turkey)
3. اَرمنستان (**armanestaan**: Armenia)
4. آذَربایجان (**aazarbaayjaan**: Azerbaijan)
5. تُرکَمَنستان (**torkamanestaan**: Turkmenistan)
6. اَفغانستان (**afghaanestaan**: Afghanistan)
7. پاکِستان (**paakestaan**: Pakistan)
8. عُمّان (**ommaan**: Oman)
9. اِمارات (**emaaraat**: Emirates)
10. قَطَر (**ghatar**: Qatar)
11. بَحرین (**bahreyn**: Bahrain)
12. عَرَبِستان (**arabestaan**: Saudi Arabia)
13. کُویت (**koveyt**: Kuwait)

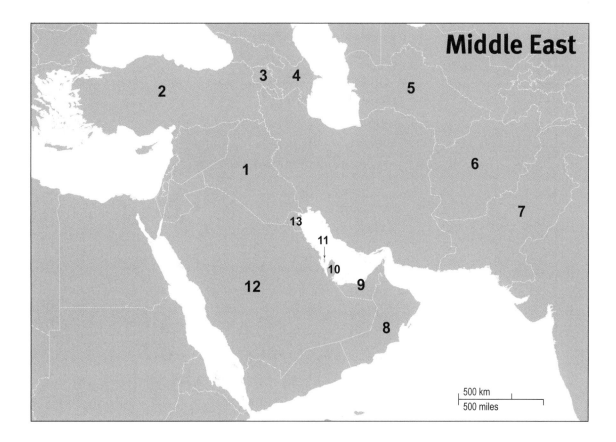

Africa

Below is a list of the countries in Africa, sorted by region. Listen to audio A03-02 to familiarize yourself with their names in Farsi.

1. آفریقا   (**aafreeghaa**: Africa)
2. اِتیوپی   (**eteeopee**: Ethiopia)
3. تانزانیا   (**taanzaaneeaa**: Tanzania)
4. کنیا   (**keneeyaa**: Kenya)
5. اوگَاندا   (**oogaanda**: Uganda)
6. موزامبیک   (**mozaambeek**: Mozambique)
7. ماداگاسکار   (**maadaagaaskaar**: Madagascar)
8. مالاوی   (**maalaavee**: Malawi)
9. زامبیا   (**zaambeeya**: Zambia)
10. زیمباوه   (**zeembavve**: Zimbabwe)
11. سومالی   (**soomaalee**: Somalia)
12. سودان جُنوبی   (**soodane jonoobee**: South Sudan)
13. رواندا   (**rooaandaa**: Rwanda)

14. بوروندی (**booroondee**: Burundi)

15. اِریتره (**ereetre**: Eritrea)

16. موریس (**moorees**: Mauritius)

17. جیبوتی (**jeebootee**: Djibouti)

18. کومور (**komor**: Comoros)

19. سیشل (**seeshel**: Seychelles)

20. جُمهوری دِموکراتیک کُنگو (**jomhooreeye demokrateeke kongo**: Democratic Republic of Congo)

21. آنگُولا (**aangoolaa**: Angola)

22. کامرون (**kaameron**: Cameroon)

23. چاد (**chaad**: Chad)

24. جُمهوری کُنگو (**jomhooreeye** Kongo)

25. جُمهوری آفریقای مَرکزی (**jomhooreeye aafreeghaaye markazee**: Central African Republic)

26. گابون (**gaabon**: Gabon)

27. گینه اُستُوایی (**geeneye ostovaayee**: Equatorial Guinea)

28. سائوتومه و پرنسیپ (**saaotome va pranseep**: Saotome and Principe)

29. مصر (**mesr**: Egypt)

30. اَلجزایر (**aljazaayer**: Algeria)

31. سودان (**soodaan**: Sudan)

32. مَراکش (**maraakesh**: Morocco)

33. تونس (**toones**: Tunisia)

34. لیبی (**leebee**: Libya)

35. آفریقای جُنوبی (**aafreeghaaye jonoobee**: South Africa)

36. نامیبیا (**naameebeeyaa**: Namibia)

37. بوتسوانا (**botsovaanaa**: Botswana)

38. لسوتو (**lesoto**: Lesotho)

39. سوازیلند (**sooazeeland**: Swaziland)

40. نیجریه (**neejereeye**: Nigeria)

41. غَنا (**ghanaa**: Ghana)

42. ساحِل عاج (**saahele aaj**: Côte d'Ivoire)

43. نیجر (**neejer**: Niger)

44. بورکینا فاسو (**boorkeena faaso**: Burkina Faso)

45. مالی (**maalee**: Mali)

46. سنگال (**senegaal**: Senegal)

47. گینه (**geene**: Guinea)

48. بنین (**beneen**: Benin)

49. توگو (**togo**: Togo)

50. سِيرا لِئون   (**seeyera leon**: Sierra Leone)
51. لِيبريا   (**leebereeya**: Liberia)
52. موريتَانی   (**mooreetaanee**: Mauritania)
53. گامبیا   (**gaambeeyaa**: Gambia)
54. گینه بیسائو   (**geeneeye beesaao**: Guinea-Bissau)
55. کیپ ورد   (**keyp verd**: Cape Verde)

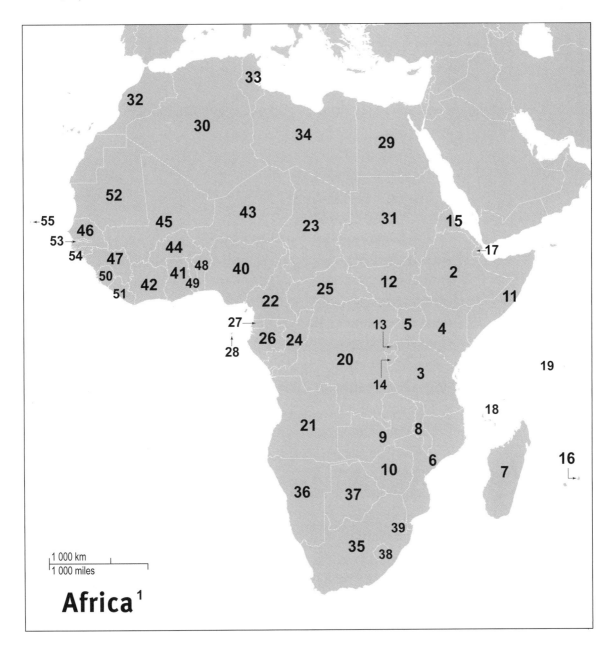

Africa[1]

Exercise 3.1   Listen to audio A03-03 and transcribe the country names.

_____ ۲.   _____ ۱.

_____ ۴.   _____ ۳.

Asia

Below is a list of the countries in Asia, sorted by region. Listen to audio A03-04 to familiarize yourself with their names in Farsi.

1. آسیا   (**aaseeyaa**: Asia)
2. تُرکیه   (**torkeeye**: Turkey)
3. عراق   (**araagh**: Iraq)
4. عَرَبِستان سعودی   (**arabestaane so'oodee**: Saudi Arabia)
5. یَمَن   (**yaman**: Yemen)
6. سوریه   (**sooreeye**: Syria)
7. اُردُن   (**ordon**: Jordan)
8. آذربایجان   (**aazarbaayjaan**: Azerbaijan)
9. اِمارات   (**Emaaraat**: Emirates)
10. اِسراییل   (**esraaeel**: Israel)
11. لُبنان   (**lobnaan**: Lebanon)
12. فلسطین   (**felesteen**: Palestine)
13. عُمّان   (**ommaan**: Oman)
14. کُویت   (**Koveyt**: Kuwait)
15. گُرجِستان   (**gorjestaan**: Georgia)
16. اَرمَنِستان   (**armanestan**: Armenia)
17. قطر   (**ghatar**: Qatar)
18. بَحرین   (**bahreyn**: Bahrain)
19. قبرس   (**ghebres**: Cypress)
20. هِندوسِتان   (**hendoostaan**: India)
21. پاکستان   (**paakestaan**: Pakistan)
22. بَنگلادش   (**baglaadesh**: Bangladesh)
23. ایران   (**eeraan**: Iran)
24. اَفغانِستان   (**afghaanestaan**: Afghanistan)

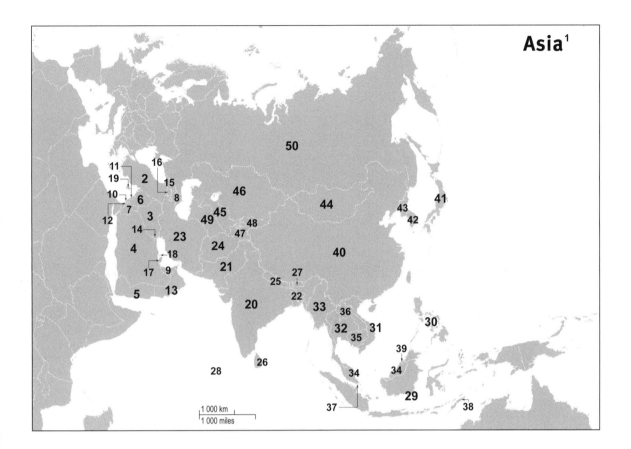

Asia[1]

25. نِپال	(**nepaal**: Nepal)
26. سِریلانکا	(**seree laankaa**: Sri Lanka)
27. بوتان	(**bootaan**: Bhutan)
28. مالدیو	(**maaldeev**: Maldives)
29. اَندونِزی	(**andoonezee**: Indonesia)
30. فیلیپین	(**feeleepeen**: Philippines)
31. ویتَنام	(**veeyetnaam**: Vietnam)
32. تایَلند	(**taayland**: Thailand)
33. میانمار	(**meeyaanmaar**: Myanmar)
34. مالِزی	(**maalezee**: Malaysia)
35. کامبوج	(**kaaboj**: Cambodia)
36. لائوس	(**laaoos**: Laos)
37. سَنگاپور	(**sangaapoor**: Singapore)
38. تیمور	(**teemor**: Timor)
39. برونئی	(**broneyee**: Brunei)
40. چین	(**cheen**: China)
41. ژاپُن	(**zhaapon**: Japan)

42. کُره جُنوبی	(**koreye jonoobi**: South Korea)
43. کُره شُمالی	(**koreye shomali**: North Korea)
44. مُغولستان	(**mogholestaan**: Mongolia)
45. اُزبَکستان	(**ozbakestaan**: Uzbekistan)
46. قَزّاقستان	(**ghazzaaghestaan**: Kazakhstan)
47. تاجیکستان	(**taajeekestaan**: Tajikistan)
48. قرقیزستان	(**ghergheezestaan**: Kyrgyzstan)
49. تُرکَمَنِستان	(**torkamanestaan**: Turkmenistan)
50. روسیه	(**rooseeye**: Russia)

Exercise 3.2   Listen to audio A03-05 and transcribe it.

٢. _____   ١. _____

٤. _____   ٣. _____

Europe

Below is a list of the countries in Europe, sorted by region. Listen to audio A03-06 to familiarize yourself with their names in Farsi.

1. اُروپا	(**oroopa**: Europe)
2. روسیه	(**rooseeye**: Russia)
3. اوکراین	(**ookraayn**: Ukraine)
4. لَهستان	(**lahestaan**: Poland)
5. رومانی	(**romaanee**: Romania)
6. چک	(**chek**: Czechia)
7. مَجارستان	(**majaarestaan**: Hungary)
8. بِلاروس	(**belaaroos**: Belarus)
9. بُلغارِستان	(**bolghaarestaan**: Bulgaria)
10. اُسلُواکی	(**oslovaakee**: Slovakia)
11. مولداوی	(**moldaavee**: Moldova)
12. بریتانیا	(**breetaaneeyaa**: The United Kingdom)
13. سوئد	(**sooed**: Sweden)
14. دانمارک	(**daanmaark**: Denmark)
15. فَنلاند	(**fanlaand**: Finland)
16. نُروژ	(**norvezh**: Norway)

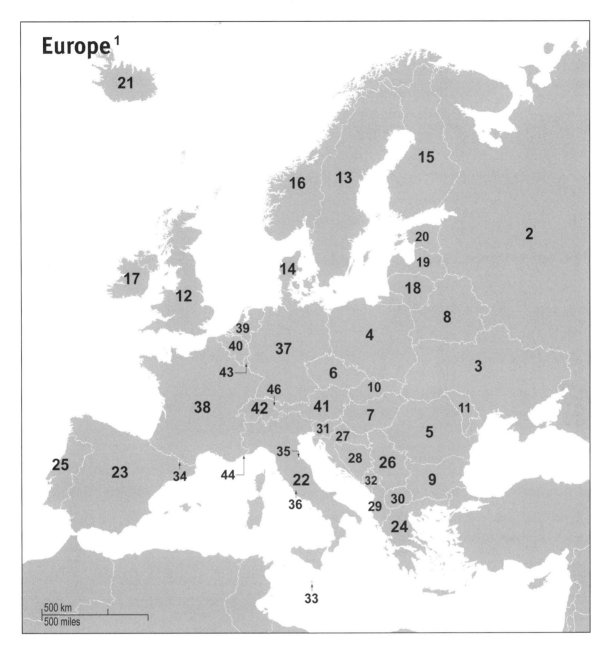

Europe[1]

17. ايرلَند (**eerland**: Ireland)

18. ليتوانى (**leetooaanee**: Lithuania)

19. لاتويا (**laatveeyaa**: Latvia)

20. إستونى (**estonee**: Estonia)

21. ايسلَند (**eesland**: Iceland)

22. ايتاليا (**eetaaleeyaa**: Italy)

23. إسپانيا (**espaaneeyaa**: Spain)

24. يونان (**yoonaan**: Greece)

25. پُرتُغال	(**portoghaal**: Portugal)
26. صربستان	(**serbestaan**: Serbia)
27. کُرُواسی	(**krovaasee**: Croatia)
28. بوسنی وَ هِرزگوین	(**bosnee va herzegoveen**: Bosna and Herzegovina)
29. آلبانی	(**aalaabee**: Albany)
30. مَقدونیه شُمالی	(**maghdooneeyeye shomalee**: North Macedonia)
31. اِسلوُنی	(**eslovonee**: Eslovenia)
32. مونته نگرو	(**monte negro**: Montenegro)
33. مالت	(**malt**: Malta)
34. آندورا	(**aandoraa**: Andorra)
35. سان مارینو	(**saan maarino**: San Marino)
36. واتیکان	(**vaateekaan**: Holy See)
37. آلمان	(**aalmaan**: Germany)
38. فَرانسه	(**faraanse**: France)
39. هُلَند	(**holand**: Netherlands)
40. بِلژیک	(**belzheek**: Belgium)
41. اُتریش	(**otreesh**: Austria)
42. سویس	(**sooees**: Switzerland)
43. لوکزامبورگ	(**lookzaamboorg**: Luxembourg)
44. موناکو	(**monaako**: Monaco)
45. لیختِن اِشتایِن	(**likhteneshtaayn**: Liechtenstein)

Exercise 3.3   Listen to audio A03-07 and transcribe it.

_____ ۲.   _____ ۱.

_____ ۴.   _____ ۳.

The Americas

Below is a list of the countries in the Americas, sorted by region. Listen to audio A03-08 to familiarize yourself with their names in Farsi.

1. آمریکا	(**aamreekaa**: Americas)
2. کانادا	(**kaanaadaa**: Canada)
3. آمریکا	(**aamreekaa**: USA)

1 000 km
1 000 miles

Americas[1]

4.	کوبا	(**koobaa**: Cuba)
5.	هائیتی	(**haa'eetee**: Haiti)
6.	جُمهوری دومنیکن	(**jomhooreeye domeneecan**: Dominican Republic)
7.	جامائیکا	(**jaamaaeekaa**: Jamaica)
8.	ترینیداد و توباگو	(**tereeneedaad va tobaago**: Trinidad and Tobago)
9.	باهاما	(**baahaamaa**: Bahamas)
10.	باربادوس	(**baarbaados**: Barbados)
11.	سَنت لوسیا	(**sant looseeyaa**: Saint Lucia)
12.	سَنت وینسِنت وَ گِرِنادین	(**sant veensent va gerenaadeen**: St. Vincent and Grenadine)
13.	گِرنادا	(**gerenaada**: Grenada)
14.	آنتیگوا وَ بارَبودا	(**aanteegooaa va baarbooda**: Antigua and Barbuda)
15.	دومینیکا	(**domeeneekaa**: Dominica)
16.	سَنت کیتس وَ نِویس	(**sant keets va nevees**: Saint Kitts and Nevis)
17.	مکزیک	(**mekzeek**: Mexico)
18.	گواتِمالا	(**gooaatemaalaa**: Guatemala)
19.	هُندوراس	(**hondooraas**: Honduras)
20.	اِلسالوادور	(**elsaalvaador**: El Salvador)
21.	نیکاراگوئه	(**neekaaraagooe**: Nicaragua)
22.	کوستاریکا	(**kostaareeka**: Costa Rica)
23.	پاناما	(**paanaamaa**: Panama)
24.	بلیز	(**beleez**: Belize)
25.	بِرزیل	(**berezeel**: Brazil)
26.	کُلمبیا	(**kolombeeya**: Colombia)
27.	آرژانتین	(**aarzhanteen**: Argentina)
28.	پرو	(**peroo**: Peru)
29.	وِنزوئلا	(**venezooela**: Venezuela)
30.	شیلی	(**sheelee**: Chile)
31.	اِکوادور	(**ekooador**: Ecuador)
32.	بولیوی	(**boleevee**: Bolivia)
33.	پاراگوئه	(**paaraagooe**: Paragua)
34.	اوروگوئه	(**orogooe**: Uruguay)
35.	گویان	(**gooyaan**: Guyana)
36.	سورینام	(**sooreenaam**: Surinam)

Exercise 3.4 Listen to audio A03-09 and transcribe what you hear in Farsi.

‏.۲ _____   ‏.۱ _____

‏.۴ _____   ‏.۳ _____

Australia and Oceania

Below is a list of the countries in Australia and the Oceania, sorted by region. Listen to audio A03-10 to familiarize yourself with their names in Farsi.

1. ‏اُسترالیا وَ اُقیانوسیه   (**ostoraleeyaa va oghyaanooseeye**: Australia and Oceania)
2. ‏اُسترالیا   (**ortoraleea**: Australia)
3. ‏زلاندنو   (**zelaandeno**: New Zealand)
4. ‏پاپواگینه نو   (**paapooaa geeneye no**: Papua New Guinea)

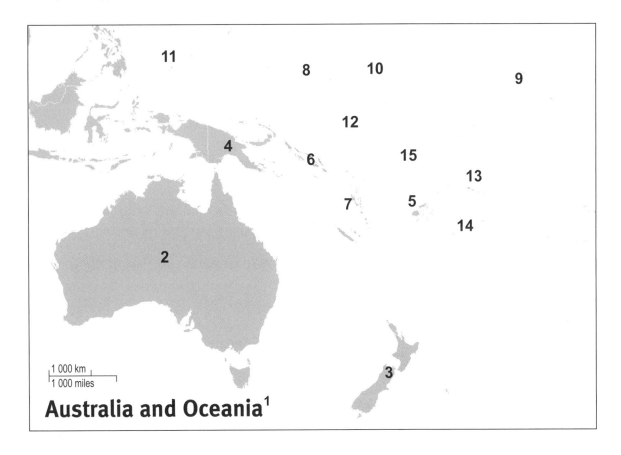

Australia and Oceania[1]

5. فيجى   (**feejee**: Fiji)

6. جَزايرِ سُليمان   (**jazaayere soleymaan**: Solomon Islands)

7. وانواتو   (**vaanooaatoo**: Vanuatu)

8. ميكرونزى   (**meekronezee**: Micronesia)

9. كيريباسى   (**keereebaasee**: Kiribati)

10. جَزايرِ مارشال   (**jazaayere maarshaal**: Marshall Islands)

11. پالائو   (**paalaaoo**: Palau)

12. نائورو   (**naaooroo**: Nauru)

13. ساموا   (**Saamoaa**: Samoa)

14. تونگا   (**tongaa**: Tonga)

15. توالو   (**toovaaloo**: Tuvalu)

North and South Pole

Listen to audio A03-11 to get familiar with the pronunciation of the North and South Pole.

قُطب شُمال   (**ghotbe shomal**: North Pole)

قُطب جُنوب   (**ghotbe jonoob**: South Pole)

Exercise 3.5   Listen to audio A03-12 and transcribe what you hear in Farsi.

_____ .۲   _____ .۱

_____ .۴   _____ .۳

Family and Relatives

Like most traditional countries, family and relatives are an important part of the Iranians' lives. Maybe that is why each family relation has a name. Listen to audio A03-13 to familiarize yourself with the following family members.

پدَر   (**pedar**: father)   بابا   (**baabaa**: dad)

مادَر   (**maadar**: mother)   مامان   (**maamaan**: mom)

بَرادَر   (**baraadar**: brother)   خواهَر   (**khaahar**: sister)

هَمسَر   (**hamsar**: spouse, no gender)   شوهَر   (**shohar**: husband)

زَن   (**zan**: wife)

Grandparents

Listen to audio A03-14 to familiarize yourself with the pronunciation of grandparents and children/ grandchildren in Farsi.

پدربُزُرگ (**pedarbozorg**: grandfather)

بَابا بُزُرگ (**bababozorg**: grandpa)

مادَربُزُرگ (**maadarbozorg**: grandmother)

مامان بُزُرگ (**maamaanbozorg**: grandma)

Children and Grandchildren

فَرزَند (**farzand**: child, as one's child)

دُختَر (**dokhtar**: daughter)

پِسَر (**pesar**: son)

نَوه (**nave**: grandchild)

Aunts and Uncles

In Farsi each aunt and uncles have their own specific name depending on whether they are on the paternal or maternal. Similarly, the gender of cousins is also specified, in addition to their relationship to the speaker. Listen to audio A03-15 to get familiar with the pronunciation of aunts, uncles, and cousins in Farsi.

خاله (**khaale**: maternal aunt, mother's sister)

پسَرخاله (**pesar khaale**: male cousin, maternal aunt's son)

دُختَرخاله (**dokhtar khale**: female cousin, maternal aunt's daughter)

عَمّه (**ammeh**: paternal aunt, father's sister)

پسَرعَمّه (**pesar amee**: male cousin, paternal aunt's son)

دُختَرعَمّه (**dokhtar amme**: female cousin, paternal aunt's daughter)

دایی (**daayee**: maternal uncle, mother's brother)

پسَردایی (**pesar daayee**: male cousin, maternal uncle's son)

دُختَردایی (**dokhtar daayee**: female cousin, paternal uncle's daughter)

عَمو (**amoo**: paternal uncle, father's brother)

پسَرعَمو (**pesar amoo**: male cousin, paternal uncle's son)

دُختَرعَمو (**dokhtar amoo**: female cousin, paternal uncle's daughter)

Nieces and Nephews

In Farsi, nieces and nephews do not have gender-specific terms like they do in English. Instead we specify if they are the child of a brother or a sister. Listen to audio A03-16 to familiarize yourself with the pronunciation of niece and nephew in Farsi.

خواهَرزاده   (**khaaharzade**: niece or nephew, word by word: sister's child)

بَرادَرزاده   (**baraadarzade**: niece or nephew, word by word: brother's child)

In-Laws

Just like the aunts/uncles, the in-law relationships are also specified. Listen to audio A03-16 to familiarize yourself with the pronunciation of the in-law terms in Farsi.

عَروس   (**aroos**: daughter-in-law)

داماد   (**daamaad**: son-in-law)

زَن بَرادَر   (**zan baraadar**: brother in law, literally means brother's wife)

شوهَرخواهَر   (**shohar khaahar**: literally means sister's husband)

جارى   (**jaaree**: relationship between a woman and her brother-in-law's wife)

باجِناق   (**bajenaagh**: relationship between a man and his sister-in-law's husband)

Exercise 3.6   Translate the following family relationships to Farsi.

1.   Grandfather   _____

2.   Son   _____

3.   Sister-in-law's husband _____

4.   Paternal aunt   _____

5.   Sister's child (niece or nephew) _____

6. Brother-in-law   _____

7. Daughter   _____

8. Grandchild   _____

Parts of the Body

In Farsi, some of the body parts are named slightly different from in English. Look at the list of body parts below and listen to audio A03-17 to familiarize yourself with the pronunciation of the parts of the body.

سَر (**sar**: head)

مو (**moo**: hair)

اَبرو (**abroo**: eyebrow)

بینی (**beenee**: nose)

دَست (**dast**: arm + hand, whole limb)

اَنگشت (**angosht**: finger, toe)

پا (**paa**: leg + foot, whole limb)

ران (**raan**: thigh)

گَردَن (**gardan**: neck)

شکم (**shekam**: belly)

کَمَر (**kamar**: lower back)

صورَت (**soorat**: face)

چشم (**cheshm**: eye)

گوش (**goosh**: ear)

دَهان (**dahaan**: mouth)

بازو (**baazoo**: arm)

زانو (**zaanoo**: knee)

بَدَن (**badan**: body)

پُشت (**posht**: back)

باسَن (**baasan**: hips)

Exercise 3.7 Look at the image below and write the part of the body in Farsi.

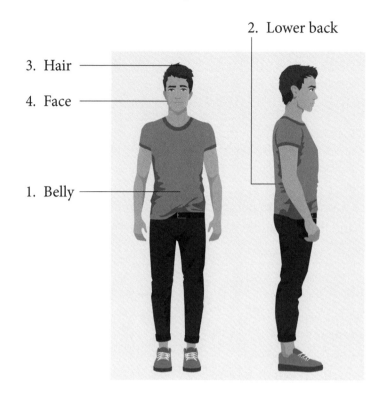

2. Lower back

3. Hair

4. Face

1. Belly

_____ .۲   _____ .۱

_____ .۴   _____ .۳

Weather

Listen to audio A03-18 to familiarize yourself with weather related vocabulary in Farsi.

هَوا	(**havaa**: weather)	آب و هَوا	(**aab o havaa**: climate)
آفتاب	(**aaftaab**: sun)	ابر	(**abr**: cloud)
مه	(**meh**: fog)	بِاران	(**baaraan**: rain)
بَرف	(**barf**: snow)	تَگَرگ	(**tagarg**: hail)
کولاک	(**koolaak**: blizzard)	خُشک	(**khoshk**: dry)
مَرطوب	(**martoob**: humid)	گرم	(**garm**: warm, hot)

سَرد	(**sard**: cold)	خُنَک	(**khonak**: cool)
باد	(**baad**: wind)	نَسیم	(**naseem**: breeze)
طوفان	(**toofaan**: storm)	آفتابی	(**aaftaabi**: sunny)
أبری	(**abree**: cloudy)	طوفانی	(**toofaanee**: stormy)
بارانی	(**baaraanee**: rainy)	مِه آلود	(**meh aalood**: foggy)

At the Grocery Store

Listen to audio A03-19 to get familiar with food related vocabulary and short sentences in Farsi.

میوه	**meeve**: fruit	سَبزی	**sabzee**: vegetable
گوشت	**goosht**: meat	مُرغ	**morgh**: chicken
ماهی	**maahee**: fish	سیب	**seeb**: apple
پُرتُقال	**portoghaal**: orange	موز	**moz**: banana
آناناس	**aanaanaas**: pineapple	سیب زمینی	**seeb zameenee**: potato
گوجه فَرَنگی	**goje farangee**: tomato	کیلو	**keeloo**: kilo

کیلویی چند؟	**keelooyee chand?**:	How much is it a kilo?
چَنده؟	**chande?**:	How much is it?
یک کیلو لطفاً!	**yek keeloo lotfan!**:	One kilo, please!
دو کیلو لطفاً!	**do keeloo lotfan!**:	Two kilos, please!
تومان، تومَن	**toomaan/toman**:	Iranian currency
بِفَرمایید!	**Befarmaayeed!**:	Here you are!

Exercise 3.8   Listen to audio A03-20 and answer the following questions.

1.   What did the woman want to buy?   _____

2.   How much was the item?   _____

3.   How much did she buy?   _____

At the Persian Restaurant

Listen to audio A03-21 to familiarize yourself with some of the vocabulary and short sentences used in restaurants. First, listen to the whole thing several times, and then listen to each word/clause, pause, and repeat the word. Practice several times while paying attention to the pronunciation.

منو	**meno**: menu
پُرس	**pors**: portion
چُلوکباب	**cholokabaab**: kabob served over steamed rice
سالاد	**saalaad**: salad
نوشابه	**nooshaabe**: soda
ناهار	**naahaar**: lunch
شام	**shaam**: dinner
چای	**chaay**: tea
انعام	**an'aam**: tip
صورَتحساب	**soorathesaab**: check
چی میل دارید؟	**chee mey daareed?**: What would you like to have?
خوش آمدید!	**Khosh aamadeed!**: Welcome!

Exercise 3.9   Listen to audio A03-22 and answer the questions.

1.   What did the woman order? Provide two details.   _____

2.   What meal time was it?   _____

Animals

Listen to audio A03-23 to familiarize yourself with some animal names.

سَگ **sag**: dog   گُربه **gorbe**: cat

موش **moosh**: mouse   مُرغ **morgh**: chicken, hen

جوجه **jooje**: chick   خُروس **khoroos**: rooster

کبوتَر **kabootar**: pigeon   کلاغ **kalaagh**: crow

Exercise 3.10   Look at the pictures below and write the name of the animals in Farsi.

_____ .٢   _____ .١

_____ .۴   _____ .٣

Exercise 3.11   Listen to audio A03-24 several times and answer the following questions.

1.   What is the speaker's name?   _____

2.   What animal is her pet? What's the pet's name?   _____

Basic Sentences and Grammar

In this section the basic sentence structure is discussed integrated with language production.

Greetings

Audio A04-01 is a short greeting dialog. Listen to it several times. Then listen to each sentence, pause, and repeat what you heard. Try to read the text below while listening.

– سَلام مَریَم! خوبی؟

Salaam Maryam! Khhobee? (Hi Maryam! Are you doing well? / How are you?)

– مِرسی عَلی. تو چِطوری؟

Mersi Alee. To chetoree? (Thanks, Ali. How about you?)

– خوبَم.

Khoobam. (I'm good.)

– خُداحافِظ!

Khodahaafez! (Bye!)

– خُداحافِظ!

Khodahaafez! (Bye!)

Sentence Components

The basic sentence components in Farsi are similar to English, only with a different order. They are: subject, object, verb, and adverbs.

Subject

The **subject** is the same in Farsi and English. In simple terms, a subject is a noun or a clause that performs the verb action. It is what/whom the sentence is about.

Example 1 *Janet ate the ice cream.*

In this sentence, Janet performed the action of eating. Therefore, Janet is the subject.

Example 2 *The tree is tall.*

In this sentence, there is no action, but the verb describes something about the tree. So, the subject is the tree.

In most Farsi sentences, the sentence starts with a subject.

Verb

A **verb** is a word that states action. In example 1, *ate* is the verb because it states what was done. In example 2 *is* is the verb because it reflects the state of the tree. Unlike English, in Farsi it is often preferred to place the verb at the end of a sentence. Verbs are conjugated to six persons in Farsi, which will be discussed in this section. Keep in mind that there is no gender in Farsi verbs.

Object

An **object** is a noun or a clause an action has acted upon. In example 1, *ice cream* is the object because the action of eating has been performed on it. But in example 2 there is no object because *being* is no action but a description about the subject. In simple sentences in Farsi, we tend to see objects after the subject and before the verb.

Adverb

Adverbs modify adjectives, verbs, or other adverbs. Adverbs can be used to add information about a word's quality, time, place, cause, etc.

Example 3 *I go to school every day.*

In example 3 *every day* is the adverb because it tells us when the verb happens. In Farsi adverbs often come after the subject.

The sentence order below works oftentimes. However, in Farsi grammar rules are not followed very strictly.

Subject + Adverb + Object + Verb

Adverb Examples

Below is a list of frequently used adverbs. Listen to audio A04-02 to familiarize yourself with their pronunciations.

اینجا	**eenjaa**: here	آنجا	**aanjaa**: there
خیلی	**kheylee**: very, so much	همیشه	**hameeshe**: always
معمولاً	**ma'moolan**: usually	اَغلَب	**aghlab**: often
گاهی	**gaahee**: sometimes	هَرگِز	**hargez**: never

Pluralization

In Farsi, there are several ways to pluralize. We will discuss two of the most frequently used methods in this book. They are the two suffixes: ها **haa** and ان **aan**.

ها **haa**

ها can be added to every word to make it plural. Look at the examples below and listen to audio A04-03 to familiarize yourself with their pronunciations.

كِتاب	**ketaab** (book)	كتاب ها	**ketaabhaa** (books)
دَست	**dast** (hand)	دَست ها	**dasthaa** (hands)
زَن	**zan** (woman)	زَن ها	**zanhaa** (women)
پِسَر	**pesar** (boy, son)	پِسرها	**pesarhaa** (boys, sons)

ان **aan**

The ان suffix is often used for animate (or living) objects in written Farsi. Note that this rule is not firm. Look at the examples below and listen to audio A04-04 to familiarize yourself with their pronunciations.

مُعَلِّم	**mo'allem**: teacher	مُعَلِّمان	**moallemaan**: teachers
كارگَر	**kaargar**: worker	كارگِران	**kaargaraan**: workers
دِرَخت	**derakht**; tree	دِرَختان	**derakhtaan**: trees

When the word ends in a vowel like ه, or و, an additional letter is added before the ان suffix for ease of pronunciation.

Ending in ه: Plural suffix will be گان and the ه is omitted.
Ending in و: Plural suffix will be ـیان .

Listen to audio A04-05 to familiarize yourself with their pronunciations.

دانِشجو	**daaneshjoo**: (college) student	دانِشجویان	**daaneshjooyaan**: (college) students
سِتاره	**setaare**: star	سِتارگان	**setaaregann**: stars
مُرده	**morde**: dead	مُردگان	**mordegaan**: the dead

Exercise 4.1 Pluralize the following using ها or ان.

			Plural
student	**daanesh aamooz**	دانش آموز	
man	**mard**	مَرد	
book	**ketaab**	کِتاب	
hand	**dast**	دَست	
word	**vaazheh**	واژه	
wood	**choob**	چوب	

Demonstrative Adjectives

Demonstrative adjectives are *this* and *that*. In Farsi, there are singular and plural forms of demonstrative adjectives, similar to English. However, the grammar is different.

این	**een**	this	آن	**aan**	that
اینها	**eenhaa**	these	آنها	**aanhaa**	those

One difference is that when we point at something without mentioning a name, we pluralize the demonstrative adjectives, but not the noun.

Examples

اینها سیب هَستَند.
eenhaa seeb hastand.: These are apples.

آنها بَچّه هَستَند.
aanhaa bache hastand.: Those are children.

The other difference is when we point and mention the names (like "these books" or "those children"), the demonstrative adjective is not pluralized.

Examples

این کتاب ها   **een ketaab ha**: these books
(این singular, کِتابها plural)

آن بَچّه ها   **aan bacheha**: those children
(آن singular, بَچّهها plural)

Exercise 4.2   Use a demonstrative adjective for each one of the examples below.

Example

اینها اَنار هَستَند.   **eenhaa anaar hastand**.: These are pomegranates.

این اَنارها   **een anaarha**: these pomegranates

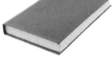

1.   Pencils: _____

2.   A book: _____

3.   Two hands: _____

4.   Five students: _____

بودَن Verb
Boodan: To be

In Farsi, one of the most commonly used verbs is بودَن (**boodan**: to be). As mentioned earlier, verbs are conjugated to six persons. There is also no gender in the Farsi verbs. They are the following persons.

1. I	2. You (singular)	3. He/She (no gender)
4. We	5. You (plural)	6. They (no gender)

The verb بودَن in simple present tense is conjugated as follows:

(I) am	**hastam**	هَستَم	(we) are	**hasteem**	هستیم
(you, singular) are	**hastee**	هَستی	(you, plural) are	**hasteed**	هستید
(he/she) is	**hast**	هَست	(they) are	**hastand**	هَستَند

Since Farsi verbs are conjugated to persons, they not only inform about the action, they tell us who did it. In other words, the subject is implied in the verbs in the form of a pronoun. We do not always have a clear subject in the sentences because it is in the verb already.

Listen to audio A04-06 to familiarize yourself with their pronunciation of the بودَن conjugation. Listen several times and try to memorize the conjugation for each person.

(I) am	**hastam**	هَستَم	(we) are	**hasteem**	هستیم
(you, singular) are	**hastee**	هَستی	(you, plural) are	**hasteed**	هستید
(he/she) is	**hast**	هَست	(they) are	**hastand**	هَستَند

أَست ast vs. هَست hast

أَست is a variation of هَست but with a different meaning. Usually هَست means "there is", while أَست means "is".

For example, the sentence غَذا هَست., means "there is food." But the sentence غَذا لَذیذ أَست. means "the food is good/delicious."

Note that this difference in meaning is only applied to the third person singular (he/she/it) and for other conjugations of the verb بودَن the same verb is used for both "is" and "there is."

Pronouns

Pronouns are words that substitute nouns or noun phrases.

Example 4   *I am happy.*

Example 5   *John is at home. He is watching TV.*

In example 4, *I* is a pronoun. In example 5, *he* is the pronoun replacing the noun *John* and referring to him.

In Farsi, there are both detached and attached pronouns. Detached pronouns are used standalone in the sentence, as the name suggests, while attached pronouns are joined to the end of nouns or other words. In this book, we will only review detached pronouns.

Detached Pronouns

In Farsi, there are six pronouns just like verb conjugation. They are:

I	**man**	مَن	we	**maa**	ما
you (singular)	**to**	تو	you (plural)	**shomaa**	شُما
he/she (no gender)	**oo**	او	they	**eeshaan/aanhaa**	ایشان/آنها

Listen to audio A04-07 to familiarize yourself with the pronunciations of the detached pronouns.

Short Dialog

Listen to audio A04-08 a couple of times and try to understand what is said.

‫ـ سَلام! مَن سارا هَستم. تو کی هَستی؟‬

‫ـ سَلام! مَن اَمیر هَستم. حالِت چِطوره؟‬

‫ـ خوب. تو خوبی؟‬

‫ـ مِرسی!‬

Now look at the transcription while listening to the audio to see what you could understand from the dialogue.

– سَلام! مَن سارا هَستم. تو کی هَستی؟

salaam! man saaraa hastam. to kee hastee? (Hi! I am Sarah. Who are you?)

– سَلام! مَن اَمیر هَستم. حالِت چِطوره؟

salaam! man ameer hastam. haalet chetore? (Hi! I am Amir. How are you?)

– خوب. تو خوبی؟

khoob! to khoobee? (Good! How about you? (word by word: Are you good?))

– مِرسی!

mersee! (Thanks!)

Exercise 4.3 Use the information given and formulate a Farsi sentences with this structure: "Mary is a dancer."

1. مینا (**meena**: a feminine name)
   دانِشجو (**daaneshjoo**: college student)   _____

2. فَرید (**fareed**: a masculine name)
   مُعَلّم (**mo'allem**: teacher)   _____

Attached بودَن (boodan: to be)

The verb بودَن has an attached form as well, which is used more frequently in spoken Farsi. Here is how it is conjugated:

ـَم (I) am	ـیم (we) are
ـی (you, singular) are	ـید (you, plural) are
ـه (he/she) is	ـَند (they) are

So, the following sentences have identical meanings.

خوب هَستیم. = خوبیم.
(we) are good.

خوب هَستَم. = خوبَم.
(I) am good.

خوب هَستید. = خوبید.
(you, plural) are good.

خوب هَستی. = خوبی.
(you, singular) are good.

خوب هَستَند. = خوبَند.
(they) are good.

خوب هَست/اَست. = خوبه.
(he/she) is good.

Listen to audio A04-09 to get familiar with the pronunciation of the attached بودَن and its conjugation in a simple sentence.

Exercise 4.4 Change the following sentences into short or long form, then translate them to English.

۱ – کارمَندَم.

۲ – عَلی خوبه.

۳ – دَر خانه تِلویزیون هَست. (تِلویزیون: TV)

۴ – خوشحالَند. (خوشحال: happy)

۵ – خانه تَمیزه. (تَمیز: clean)

۶ – موز زَرد است.

_____

_____

_____

_____

_____

_____

Verb داشتَن daashtan (to have)

The verb "to have" is conjugated in present tense the same way as بودَن (to be). We need to add the verb's present stem to the personal suffix. The present stem of داشتَن is: دار (**daar**). Therefore, it is conjugated as follows in the simple present tense:

داریم (دار+ ـیم)

دارَم (دار+ ـَم)

دارید (دار+ ـید)

داری (دار+ ـی)

دارَند (دار+ ـَند)

دارَد (دار+ ـَد)

daaram: (I) have	**daareem**: (we) have
daaree: (you, singular) have	**daareed**: (you, plural) have
daarand: (he/she) has	**daarand**: (they) have

Listen to audio A04-10 to familiarize yourself with the conjugation of داشتَن.

Review the following sentences and try to guess what they mean.

مَن اَنار دارَم.

اَمیر کِتاب دارَد.

Adjectives

An adjective is a word that modifies or describes a noun.

Example 6 *Blue pencil*

In the example *blue* is an adjective that describes the pencil.
Please note that nouns are combined with adjectives as well as other nouns.

Noun/Noun and Noun/Pronoun Combinations

Here are a few examples in English:

my book
school bus
mother's car

They have a variety of structures and names in English, but in Farsi there are three combinations of adjective/noun, noun/noun, and noun/pronoun.

Adjective/Noun, Noun/Noun, and Pronoun/Noun Combinations

In Farsi the combination of adjective/nouns and noun/nouns/pronouns are reversed compared to English. Going back to the examples above, "my book" in Farsi is literally translated as: "book of me."

کِتابِ من
Therefore, we have the "noun + of" in Farsi "+ pronoun/noun/adjective."

In Farsi there is an __ added to the last letter of the first word. Look at the following examples and pay attention to their structures. Note that then __ acts as the connector of the combined words and it can be roughly compared to the English preposition "of."

كِتاب مِن   **ketaab e man**: (literal translation) "book of me" = "my book"
اُتوبوسِ مَدرسه   **otoboos e madrese**: (literal translation) "bus of school" = "school bus"
ماشینِ مادَر   **maasheen e maadar**: (literal translation) "car of mother" = "mother's car"
مِدادِ آبی   **medaad e aabee**: (literal translation) "pencil of blue" = "blue pencil"

Variation for Nouns Ending in Vowels

If the first noun ends in a vowel like و ,ـه, and ا, a ی is added to ease pronunciation. Review the following examples:

خانه ی مِن   **khaane ye man**: my home
غذایِ علی   **ghazaa ye alee**: Ali's food
هوایِ خوب   **havaa ye khoob**: good weather

Exercise 4.5   Translate the following to Farsi. Check out the glossary at the back of the book if you do not know the Farsi translations.

1.   His school   _____

2.   Green sock   _____

3.   Yellow apple   _____

4.   Iran bank   _____

5.   White hair   _____

Exercise 4.6   Translate the following sentences to Farsi. When done, listen to audio A04-11 to check your answers.

1.   My school is here.   _____

2.   This apple is delicious. _____

3.   I am always happy.   _____

4.   Ali's book is there.   _____

Prepositions and Conjunctions

Below are the most frequently used prepositions and conjunctions in Farsi. Listen to audio A04-12 to become familiar with their pronunciations.

به	**be**: to		با	**baa**: with
وَ	**va**: and		یا	**yaa**: or
رویِ	**rooye**: on		زیرِ	**zeere**: under
بالایِ	**baalaaye**: over		دَر	**dar**: in, on, inside
اَز	**az**: from			

Exercise 4.7   look at the images below and write where each of the things is.

1.   Where is the bag?

_____

2.   Where is the cat?

_____

3.   Where is the lamp?

_____

Present Tense Personal Suffixes

Present tense personal suffixes are added to the end of the verb stem to conjugate it to different persons. This part is the implied subject. Because the verbs somehow tell you who does the action, sometimes the Farsi sentences do not have a subject, because it is implied in the verb. We will return to this topic later.

I	am	ـَم	we	eem	ـیم
you singular	ee	ی	you plural	eed	ـید
she/he	ad	ـَد	they	and	ـَند

Verb Stems

You may have noticed that in Farsi verbs have stems. These stems are the main part of the verb and by adding prefixes and suffixes we can conjugate them to various tenses and persons. Two of the verbs you have learned (داشتَن and بودَن) are exceptions, but this rule is applied to the majority of verbs.

In Farsi, there are present stems and past stems. Present stems are somewhat comparable to the English irregular verbs. The present stems need to be memorized as well since there is no rule that governs them.

Below is a list of the more frequently used verbs with their present stems. Listen to audio A04-13 to familiarize yourself with their pronunciations.

Verbs	Present Stems	بُنِ مُضارِع	فعل
raftan: to go	**ro**	رو	رَفتَن
goftan: to say	**goo**	گو	گُفتَن
deedan: to see	**been**	بین	دیدَن
khordan: to eat	**khor**	خور	خوردَن
Khaareedan: to buy	**khar**	خَر	خَریدَن
aamadan: to come	**aa (aay)**	آ (آی)	آمَدَن
kardan: to do	**kon**	کُن	کَردَن
shodan: to become	**sho**	شو	شُدَن
khaandan: to read	**khaan**	خوان	خواندَن

Simple Present Tense Conjugation

As previously discussed, the simple present tense in Farsi is conjugated as the following (read right to left):

Personal Suffix + Present Stem + می

Now let's use the above structure to conjugate the verb *(I) see* from the infinitive دیدَن.

First, add the prefix می. It is used in all simple present tense conjugations with an exception of "to be" and "to have."

Then, locate دیدَن (to go)'s present stem on the present stems table. It is: بین. Add it to می.

The last thing is to use the correct personal suffix. The verb is conjugated for "I", first person singular. The personal suffix for it is: ـَم.

Now we put them all together:

(**meebeenam**) می بینَم = ـَم + بین + می

So می بینَم means (I) see

Verbs with stems that end in a vowel change a little for ease of pronunciation in the simple present tense. The conjugations below are for the first person singular, but the change in vowel is applied to all persons.

Simple Present Tense		Infinitive	
meeravam: (I) go	می رَوَم	**raftan**: to go	رَفتن
meegooyam: (I) say	می گویَم	**goftan**: to go	گُفتَن
mee'aayam: (I) come	می آیَم	**aamadan**: to come	آمَدَن
meeshavam: (I) become	می شَوَم	**shodan**: to become	شُدَن

Listen to audios A04-14, A04-15, A04-16, and A04-17 familiarize yourself with the pronunciations and conjugations of رَفتَن (**raftan**: to go), گُفتَن (**goftan**: to say), آمَدَن (**aamadan**: to come), and شُدَن (**shodan**: to become).

meeravam: (I) go   **meeraveem**: (we) go   می رَوَم   می رَویم

meeravee: (you, singular) go   **meeraveed**: (you, plural) go   می رَوی   می رَوید

meeravad: (she/he) goes   **meeravand**: (they) go   می رَوَد   می رَوَند

meegooyam: (I) say   **meegooyeem**: (we) say   می گویَم   می گوییم

meegooyee: (you, singular) say   **meegooyeed**: (you, plural) say   می گویی   می گویید

meegooyad: (she/he) says   **meegooyand**: (they) say   می گویَد   می گویَند

meeyaayam: (I) come   **meeyaayeem**: (we) come   می آیَم   می آییم

meeyaayee: (you, singular) come   **meeyaayeed**: (you, plural) come   می آیی   می آیید

meeyaayad: (she/he) comes   **meeyaayand**: (they) come   می آیَد   می آیَند

meeshavam: (I) become   **meesahveem**: (we) become   می شَوَم   می شَویم

meeshavee: (you, singular) become   **meeshaveed**: (you, plural) become   می شَوی   می شَوید

meeshavad: (she/he) becomes   **meeshavand**: (they) become   می شَوَد   می شَوَند

Exercise 4.8   Translate the following verbs to Farsi.

1. (you, plural) see _____   2. (we) eat   _____

3. (she/he) says _____   4. (they) become   _____

5. (you, plural) buy _____   6. (I) go   _____

7. (you, singular) say_____   8. (he/she) comes   _____

Exercise 4.9   Listen to audio A04-18 and answer the questions.

1. What is the name of the speaker? _____

2. What does she often do?   _____

3. Who is Ali?   _____

4. What does Ali do?   _____

Exercise 4.10 Listen to audio A04-19 and answer the questions.

1. What color is the book? _____

2. Where is the book? _____

3. Where is the bag? _____

Questions

In Farsi to make a question, you do not need to change the sentence structure as in English. For yes/no questions you only change the sentence tone to question form and place a question mark at the end. Listen to audio A04-20 to familiarize yourself with how declarative and interrogative sentences are read.

to kaarmand hastee.: You are a clerk.

تو کارمَند هَستی.

to kaarmand hastee?: Are you a clerk?

تو کارمَند هَستی؟

bale, man kaarmand hastam.: Yes, I am a clerk.

بله، من کارمَند هستم.

na, man kaarmand neestam.: No, I am not a clerk.

نه، من کارمَند نیستم.

Exercise 4.11 Listen to audio A04-21 and answer the questions.

سلام اِلهام! خوبی؟ –

سَلام عَلی! مرسی، تو چطوری؟ –

خوبَم مرسی. الهام، تو دانِشجو هَستی؟ –

نه، من کارمَند هَستَم. –

علی، تو مُعَلّم هستی؟ –

نه، من بیکار هَستَم. –

1. What does Elham do? _____

2. What does Ali do? _____

"WH" Questions

"WH" questions are used to ask for more information. To ask "WH" questions in Farsi, you'll need to add the question word at the beginning or after the subject, change the tone to interrogative, and place a question mark at the end. Below is a list of the more common question words:

what	che	چه	who	ke / kee	که / کی
where	kojaa	کُجا	when	key	کِی
how	chetor/chegoone	چطور/ چگونه	which	kodaam	کُدام
many	How	چَند تا	much	How	چِقَدر

Exercise 4.12 Look at the images and answer the questions.

۱. چه روی کتاب است؟   ۲. که پیتزا می خورد؟

Exercise 4.13 Write a question for each underlined word like the example.

Example:

مثال: مادِر به خانه آمَد.

که به خانه آمَد؟

۱.   اَنار در بُشقاب اَست. _____

۲.   پِدَر غذا می خورَد. _____

۳.   دو کِتاب دارَم. _____

۴.   به مَدرسه می رَوَم. _____

English-Farsi Dictionary

A

Aban (eighth month of the Persian calendar)	آبان	aabaan
about	دَرباره	darbaare
absence	غِیبَت	gheybat
absent	غایب	ghaayeb
accomplice	هَمدَست	hamdast
according to	بَراَساس	bar asaas
account, calculation	حِساب	hesaab
add (v.)	اِضافه کَردَن	ezaafe kardan
additionally	به عَلاوه	be alaave
Afghanistan	اَفغانِستان	afghaanestaan
Africa	آفریقا	aafreeghaa
agency	آژانس	aazhaans
air	هَوا	havaa
air force	نیرویِ هَوایی	neeroo ye havaayee
airplane	هَواپیما	havaapeymaa
airport	فُرودگاه	foroodgaah
alcohol	اَلکُل	alkol
alcoholic drinks	مَشروب	mashroob
Ali (masculine name)	عَلی	alee
all	تَمام، کُل (هَمه)	tamaam
alley	کوچه	kooche
almond	بادام	baadaam
almost	تَقریباً	taghreeban
alone	تَنها	tanhaa
already	قَبلاً	ghablan
also	هَمچِنین، هَم	hamcheneen
always	هَمیشه	hameeshe
America	آمریکا	aamreekaa
American	آمریکایی	aamreekaayee
Amin (masculine name)	اَمین	ameen
Amir (masculine name)	اَمیر	ameer
and	وَ	va
animal	حِیوان	heyvaan
announce (v.)	اِعلام کَردَن	e'laam kardan
annual	سالانه	saalaane

answer (v.)	پاسُخ دادَن، جَواب دادَن	paasokh daadan
appealing	جَذّاب	jazzaab
apple	سیب	seeb
apply (v.)	زَدَن، به کار بُردَن	zadan
appointment	قَرار	gharaar
area	مَنطَقه	mantaghe
Aria (masculine name)	آریا	aareeyaa
arm	دَست	dast
army	اَرتش	artesh
arrow	تیر	teer
art	هُنَر	honar
article	مَقاله	maghaale
artist	هُنَرمَند	honarmand
ash	خاکِستَر	khaakestar
Asia	آسیا	aaseeyaa
artistic	هُنَری	honaree
associate degree	فوقِ دیپلُم، کاردانی	fogh e deeplom
atheism	خدانابَاوَری	khodaanaabaavaree
atheist	خُدانابَاوَر	khodaanaabaavar
atmosphere	جَو	jav
attention	تَوَجُّه	tavajjoh
attractive	جَذّاب	jazzaab
aunt (maternal)	خاله	khaale
aunt (paternal)	عَمّه	amme
authentic	اَصیل	aseel
authenticity	اِصالَت	esaalat
ax	تَبَر	tabar
Azar (ninth month of the Persian calendar)	آذر	aazar

B

bachelor's degree	کارشِناسی، لیسانس	kaarshenaasee
back	پُشت	posht
bad	بَد	bad
Bahman (eleventh month of the Persian calendar)	بَهمَن	bahman
Bahrain	بَحرین	bahreyn
banana	موز	moz

bank	بانک	baank
banknote	اِسکِناس	eskenaas
barley	جو	jo
based on	بَرَاساس	bar asaas
basket	سَبَد	sabad
battle	نَبَرد	nabard
be (v.)	بودَن	boodan
be able to	تَوانِستَن	tavaanestan
be dissolved	حَل شُدَن	hal shodan
be interested (v.)	عَلاقه داشتَن	alaaghe daashtan
beard	ریش	reesh
became	شُد	shod
because	چون	chon
become (v.)	شُدَن	shodan
bee	زَنبور	zamboor
beetle	سوسک	soosk
before	پیش، قَبل	peesh
beginning	شُروع، آغاز	shoroo'
behind	پُشت	posht
bell	زَنگ	zang
belly	شِکَم	shekam
benefit	سود	sood
best	بِهتَرین	behtareen
better	بِهتَر	behtar
between	بین	beyn
beverage	نوشابه	nooshaabe
bicycle	دوچَرخه	docharkhe
big	بُزُرگ، چاق، گُنده	bozorg
bill	صورَتحساب	soorathesaab
billion	میلیارد	meelyaard
biology	زیست شِناسی	zeest shenaasee
bird	پَرَنده	parande
birth	تَوَلُّد	tavallod
birthday	تَوَلُّد	tavallod
bitter	تَلخ	talkh
black	سیاه، مِشکی	seeyaah
black market	بازارِ سیاه	bazaar e seeyaah

blade	تیغ	teegh
blanket	پَتو	patoo
blizzard	کولاک	koolaak
blond	بور	boor
blow (v.)	فوت کَردَن	foot kardan
blue	آبی	aabee
boat	قایِق	ghaayegh
body	بَدَن، تَن، بَدَنه	badan
book	کِتاب	ketaab
born (n.)	مُتَوَلِّد	motevalled
boss	رئیس	ra'ees
bowl	کاسه	kaase
box	جَعبه	ja'be
boy	پِسَر	pesar
boyfriend	دوست پِسَر	doost pesar
brain	مَغز	maghz
bread	نان	naan
break (v.)	شِکَستَن	shekastan
breakfast	صُبحانه	sobhaane
breathe	نَفَس کِشیدَن	nafas kesheedan
breeze	نَسیم	naseem
brick oven	تَنور	tanoor
bride	عَروس	aroos
bright	روشَن	roshan
broken	خَراب	khaaraab
brother	بَرادَر	baraadar
brother-in-law (a man's wife's sister's husband)	باجِناق	baajenaagh
brother-in-law (one's sister's husband)	شوهَرخواهَر	shohar khale
brown	قَهوه‌ای	ghahve'ee
bruise	کَبود	kabood
bucket	سَطل	satl
bud (flower)	غُنچه	ghonche
Buddhism	بودیسم	boodeesm
Buddhist	بودایی	boodaayee
budget	بودجه	boojje
build (v.)	ساختَن	saakhtan

building number	پلاک (خانه)	pelaak
bullet	تیر	teer
burgundy (adj.)	شَرابی	sharaabee
bus	اُتوبوس	otoboos
bush	بوته	boote
but	اَمّا، وَلی	ammaa
butter	کَره	kare
butterfly	پَروانه	parvaane
buy (v.)	خَریدَن	khareedan
buyer	خَریدار	khareedaar
by	تا (تَوَسُّط)	taa

C

cable	سیم	seem
cage	قَفَس	ghafas
call (v.)	زَنگ زَدَن	zang zadan
calm	آرامِش	aaraamesh
came (he/she)	آمَد	aamad
camel	شُتُر	shotor
Canada	کانادا	kaanaadaa
canary	قَناری	ghanaaree
cantaloupe	طالِبی	taalebee
car	ماشین	maasheen
careful	مُواظِب	movaazeb
carnivore	گوشتخوار	gooshtkhaar
carrot	هَویج	haveej
carry (v.)	حَمل کَردَن	haml kardan
case	مورد (جَعبه)	mored
cash (v.)	نَقد کَردَن	naghd kardan
castle	قَلعه	ghal'e
cat	گُربه	gorbe
cause	باعِث	baa'es
cell phone	تِلِفُنِ هَمراه، موبایل	telefon e hamraah
center	مَرکَز	markaz
central	مَرکَزی	markazee
century	سَده، قَرن	sade
certain	مُطمَئِن	motma'en
certainly	حَتماً	hatman
certainty	اِطمینان	etmeenaan
chair	صَندَلی	sandalee
champion	قَهرَمان	ghahremaan
championship	قَهرَمانی	ghahremaanee
change	تَغییر	taghyeer
change (n.)	تَغییر کَردَن	taghyeer kardan
change something (v.)	تَغییر دادَن	taghyeer daadan
check (n.)	صورَتِحِساب، چِک	soorathesaab
cheese	پَنیر	paneer
chemistry (science)	شیمی	sheemee
cherry	گیلاس	geelaas
chewing gum	آدامس	aadaams
chick	جوجه	jooje
chicken	مُرغ	morgh
child	کودَک (بَچّه)	bachche
China	چین	cheen
china	چینی	cheenee
Chinese	چینی	cheenee
Christian (adj.)	مَسیحی	maseehee
Christianity	مَسیحیَت	maseeyeeyat
cigar	سیگارِبَرگ	seegaarbarg
cigarette	سیگار	seegaar
cinema	سینَما	seenamaa
circle	میدان، دایره	meydaan
city	شَهر	shahr
class	کِلاس	kelaas
clean	تَمیز	tameez
clerk	کارمَند	kaarmand
climate	آب و هَوا، اِقلیم	aab o havaa
clock	ساعَت، ساعَتِ دیواری	Saa'at
close (adj.)	نَزدیک	nazdeek
clothing	لِباس	lebaas
cloud	اَبر	abr
cloudy	اَبری	abree
coarse	زِبر	zebr
cockroach	سوسَک	soosk
coffee	قَهوه	ghahve

coffee shop	کافی‌شاپ	kaafeeshaap
coin	سِکّه	sekke
cold (adj.)	سَرد	sard
cold (n.)	سَرما	sarmaa
colleague	هَمکار	hamkaar
college	دانشگاه، کالِج	daaneshgaah
color	رَنگ	rang
comb (n.)	شانه	shaane
come (v.)	آمَدن	aamadan
commando	تَکاوَر	takaavar
committee	کُمیته	komeete
company	شِرکَت	sherkat
compare (v.)	مُقایسه کَردن	moghaayese kardan
comparison	مُقایسه	moghaayese
competition	مُسابقه، رِقابَت	mosaabeghe
completely	کامِلاً	kaamelan
computer	رایانه، کامپیوتر	raayaane
conclusion	نَتیجه گیری	nateeje geeree
condition	شَرط	shart
conditional	مَشروط	mashroot
conditions	شُروط	shoroot
conservative (politics)	راستگرا	raastgaraa
constantly	دایماً	daa'eman
Constitution	قانون اَساسی	ghanoon e asaasee
consumer	مَصرَف کُنَنده	masraf konnande
consumerism	مَصرَف گَرایی	masrafgaraayee
consumption	مَصرَف	masraf
contact	تَماس	tamaas
container, dish(es)	ظَرف	zarf
control (v.)	کُنتُرل کَردن	kontorol kardan
cooked	پُخته	pokhte
cool	خُنَک	khonak
cooperate (v.)	هَمکاری کَردن	hamkaaree kardan
cooperation	هَمکاری	hamkaaree
copper	مِس	mes
corn	ذُرَّت	zorrat

correct	دُرُست، صَحیح	dorost
cost	هَزینه	hazeene
could	تَوانِست	tavaanest
count (v.)	شُمُردَن	shemordan
counting	شُمارِش	shomaaresh
country	کِشوَر	keshvar
court (of law)	دادگاه	daadgaah
court (extended royal household)	دَربار	darbaar
cousin (the daughter of one's maternal aunt)	دُختَرخاله	dokhtar khaale
cousin (the daughter of one's maternal uncle)	دُختَردایی	dokhtar daayee
cousin (the daughter of one's paternal aunt)	دُختَرعَمّه	dokhtar amme
cousin (the daughter of one's paternal uncle)	دُختَرعَمو	dokhtar amoo
cousin (the son of one's maternal aunt)	پِسَرخاله	pesar khaale
cousin (the son of one's maternal uncle)	پِسَردایی	pesar daayee
cousin (the son of one's paternal aunt)	پِسَرعَمّه	pesar amme
cousin (the son of one's paternal uncle)	پِسَرعَمو	pesar amoo
crab	خَرچَنگ	kharchang
cream	خامه	khaame
crime	جُرم	jorm
criminal	مُجرِم	mojrem
crisis	بُحران	bohraan
crispy	تُرد	tord
critical	بُحرانی	bohraanee
critique (n.)	نَقد	naghd
critique (v.)	نَقد کَردن	naghd kardan
cross (n.)	صَلیب	saleeb
cross (v.)	گُذَشتَن، عُبور کَردن	gozashtan
crow	کلاغ	kalaagh
crown	تاج	taaj
crude	خام	khaam
cultural	فَرهَنگی	farhangee
culture	فَرهَنگ	farhang
cumin	زیره	zeere

cup	لیوان، فنجان	leevaan
curly	فر	fer
current (adj.)	جاری	jaaree
current year	اِمسال	emsaal
cut (v.)	قطع کَردَن، بُریدَن	ghat' kardan
cycle (v.)	دوچَرخه سَواری کردن	dochrkhe savaaree kardan

D

dad, daddy	بابا	baabaa
damage	ضَرر، آسیب	zarar
danger	خَطَر	khatar
dangerous	خَطَرناک	khatarnaak
dark	تاریک، تیره	taareek
darkness	تاریکی	taareekee
date	قَرار، تاریخ	gharaar
daughter, girl	دُختَر	dokhtar
day	روز	rooz
Day (tenth month of the Persian calendar)	دِی	dey
day care center	کودَکِستان، مَهدِکودَک	koodakestaan
dead	مُرده	morde
decade	دهه	dahe
decide	تَصمیم گِرفتَن	tasmeem gereftan
decision	تَصمیم	tasmeem
defeat (n.)	شکَست	shekast
defeat (v.)	شِکَست دادَن	shekast daadan
defense	دِفاع	defaa'
delicious	لَذیذ	lazeez
democracy	دِموکراسی	demokraasee
democrat	دِموکرات	demokraat
deposit (v.)	واریز کَردَن	vaareez kardan
desert	بیابان، صَحرا	beeyaabaan
desk	میز	meez
despite	عَلی رَغم	alaa raghm
details	جُزئیات	joz'eeyyat
determined	مُصَمَّم	mosammam
device	دَستگاه	dastgaah
diaper	پوشَک	pooshak

did	کَرد	kard
die (v.)	مُردَن	mordan
diet (v.)	رژیم گِرفتَن	rezheem gereftan
difference	تَفاوُت	tafaavot
different	مُتَفاوِت	motefaavet
dimension	بُعد	bo'd
dimensions	أبعاد	ab'aad
dinner	شام	shaam
diploma	دیپلُم	deeplom
director	رئیس، مُدیر	ra'ees
dirty	کَثیف	kaseef
disease	بیماری، مَریضی	beemaaree
dissolve (v.)	حَل کردن	hal kardan
divorced (woman)	مُطَلَّقه	motallaghe
do (v.)	أنجام دادَن، کَردَن	anjaam daadan
doctor	دُکتُر	doktor
doctorate	دکترا	doktoraa
dog	سَگ	sag
dollar	دُلار	dolaar
domestic, internal	داخِلی	daakhelee
donkey	أُلاغ	olaagh
doogh (yoghurt drink)	دوغ	doogh
door	دَر، باب	dar
doorkeeper	دَربان	darbaan
dot	نُقطه	noghte
dough	خَمیر	khameer
down	پایین	paayeen
drank	نوشید	noosheed
drink (n.)	نوشیدَنی، مَشروب	noosheedanee
drink (v.)	نوشیدَن	noosheedan
drive (v.)	رانندگی کَردن	raanandegee kardan
driver	رانَنده	raanande
drop	قَطره	ghatre
dry	خُشک	khoshk
duck	أُردَک	ordak
duck (wild)	مُرغابی	morghaabee

| duration | مُدَّت | moddat |
| during | طِی | tey |

E

each	هَر	har
each other	یِکدیگَر	yekdeegar
ear	گوش	goosh
early	زود	zood
earth	زَمین	zameen
east	شَرق	shargh
eastern	شَرقی	sharghee
easy	ساده، آسان	saade
eat (v.)	خوردَن	khordan
economy	اِقتصاد	eghtesaad
education	آموزِش	aamoozesh
effect	اَثَر، تأثیر	asar
effective	مُؤَثِّر	mo'asser
eight	هَشت	hasht
eight hundred	هَشتصَد	hashtsad
eighteen	هِجدَه	hejdah
eighty	هَشتاد	hashtaad
elections	اِنتخابات	entekhaabaat
electricity	بَرق	bargh
elementary school	دَبِستان	dabestaan
elephant	فیل	feel
eleven	یازدَه	yaazdah
Elham (feminine name)	اِلهام	elhaam
email	ایمِیل	eemeyl
Emirates (UAE)	اِمارات	emaaraat
end	آخَر، پایان، تَمام	aakhar
energy	اِنرژی	enerzhee
engine	ماشین، موتور	maasheen
English	اِنگِلیسی	engeleesee
entire	کُل	kol
entrance	وُرودی	voroodee
entry	وُرود	vorood
envelope	پاکَت	paakat

equal	بَرابَر، مُساوی	baraabar
equality	بَرابَری	baraabaree
equivalent	مُعادِل	mo'aadel
era	عَصر، دوره، زَمان، دوران	asr
Esfand (twelfth month of the Persian calendar)	اِسفَند	esfand
Europe	اُروپا	oroopaa
even	حَتّی	hattaa
evening	عَصر	asr
every	هَمه	hame
example	مِثال	mesaal
exercise	نَرمِش، وَرزِش	narmesh
exercise (v.)	نَرمِش کَردَن، وَرزِش کَردَن	narmesh kardan
existing	موجود	mojood
exit	خُروج، خُروجی	khorooj
expansion	گُستَرِش	gostaresh
expense	هَزینه	hazeene
expert	کارشِناس، مُتَخَصِّص	kaarshenaas
express (v.)	بَیان کَردَن	bayan kardan
extra	اِضافی	ezaafee
eye	چِشم	cheshm
eyeglasses	عِینَک	eynak

F

fabric	پارچه	paarche
face	صورَت	soorat
facilities	اِمکانات	emkaanaat
facing	روبِرو	rooberoo
fall in love (v.)	عاشِق شُدَن	aashegh shodan
faloodeh (Persian dessert)	فالوده	faaloode
family	خانِواده	khaanevaade
far	دور	door
Farid (masculine name)	فَرید	fareed
farm	مَزرَعه	mazra'e
farmer	کِشاوَرز	keshaavarz
farms	مَزارِع	mazaare'
Farsi	فارسی	faarsee
Farvardin (first month of the Persian calendar)	فَروَردین	farvardeen

fast	تُند، سَریع	tond
fat (adj.)	چاق	chaagh
father	پِدَر	pedar
faucet	شیر، شیرِ آب	sheer
fax	دورنگار، فاکس	doornegaar
fear	تَرس، وَحشَت	tars
feather	پَر	par
feeling	اِحساس	ehsaas
female	مادّه، زَن	maadde
fence	نَرده	narde
festival	جَشنواره، فِستیوال	jashnvaare
fever	تَب	tab
fiction	داستانی	daastaanee
field	حوزه، میدان	hoze
fifteen	پانزدَه	paanzdah
fifty	پَنجاه	panjaah
fight (n.)	مُبارزه، جَنگ	mobaareze
fight (v.)	مُبارزه کَردَن	mobareze kardan
film	فیلم	feelm
financial	مالی	maalee
finger	اَنگُشت، اَنگُشتِ دَست	angosht
fire	آتش، آتش‌سوزی، حَریق	aatash
fire fighter	مأمورآتش‌نشانی، آتش‌نِشان	ma'moor e atashneshaanee
fire station	آتش‌نِشانی	aatash neshaanee
first	اوّل	avval
first name	اِسم کوچَک	esm e koochak
fish	ماهی	maahee
fist	مُشت	mosht
fistful	مُشت	mosht
five	پَنج	panj
five hundred	پانصَد	paansad
fix (v.)	دُرست کَردَن، تَعمیر کَردَن	dorost kardan
flat	صاف، هَموار	saaf
flight (n.)	پَرواز	parvaaz
flood (n.)	سِیل	seyl
flour	آرد	aard
flower	گُل	gol
fly (n.)	مَگَس	magas
fly (v.)	پَرواز کردن	parvaaz kardan
foam	کَف	kaf
fog	مه	meh
foggy	مه آلود	mehaalood
food	غذا	ghazaa
foot	پا	paa
football	فوتبالِ آمریکایی	football aamreekaayee
for	بَرای	baraaye
for example	مَثَلاً	masalan
force (n.)	نیرو	neeroo
foreign	خارجی	khaarejee
forest	جَنگل	jangal
forgive (v.)	گُذَشتَن، بَخشیدَن	gozashtan
form (n.)	شکل	shekl
form (v.)	تَشکیل دادَن	tashkeel daadan
formula (baby food)	شیرخُشک	sheer e khoshk
forty	چِهِل	chehel
four	چهار	chaahaar
four hundred	چَهارصد	chaahaarsad
four-way	چَهارراه	chaahar rah
fourteen	چَهاردَه	chaahaardah
France	فَرانسه	faraanse
free	آزاد	aazaad
free market	بازارِ آزاد	bazaar e aazaad
freedom	آزادی	aazaadee
freedom of speech	آزادیِ بَیان	aazaadee ye bayaan
fresh	تازه	taaze
Friday	جُمعه	jom'e
friend	دوست، رَفیق	doost
friendship	دوستی، رِفاقَت	doostee
from	از	az
front	جِلو	jelo
fruit	میوه	meeve
full	پُر	por
fundamentalist	اُصولگرا	osoolgaraa
fungus	قارچ	ghaarch

furniture	أثاث	asaas
future	آینده	aayande

G

game	بازی	baazee
garage	گاراژ	gaaraazh
gardener	باغبان	baaghbaan
garlic	سیر	seer
gas (fuel)	بنزین	benzeen
gas (state of matter)	گاز	gaaz
gate	دَروازه	darvaaze
generally	به طورِ کُلّی، کُلّاً	be tore kollee
gentleman	آقا	aagha
Germany	آلمان	aalmaan
gill	آبشُش	aabshosh
giraffe	زَرّافه	zarraafe
girl	دُختَر	dokhtar
girlfriend	دوست‌دُختَر	doost dokhtar
give (v.)	دادَن	daadan
glass	لیوان، شیشه	leevaan
glue	چَسب	chasb
go (v.)	رَفتَن	raftan
Go ahead!	بِفَرمایید!	befarmaayeed
god	خُدا، الله، ایزَد	khoda
godly	باخُدا	baakhodaa
gold (n.)	طَلا، زَر	talaa
golden	طَلایی	talayee
good	خوب، خوبی، خیر	khoob
good job!	آفرین، بارک الله! (باریکّلا)	aafareen
goodbye	خُداحافظ	khodaahaafez
gossip (n.)	غیبَت	gheybat
gossip (v.)	غیبَت کَردَن	gheybat kardan
government	دولَت	dolat
governor	اُستاندار	ostaandaar
grandchild	نَوه	nave
grandfather	پدَربُزُرگ	pedarbozorg
grandma	مامان‌بُزُرگ	maamaan bozorg
grandmother	مادربُزُرگ	maadar bozorg

grandpa	بابابُزُرگ	baaba abozorg
grape(s)	اَنگور	angoor
grapevine	مو، دَرَختِ اَنگور	mo
gravity	جاذبه	jaazebe
gray	توسی، خاکِستَری	toosee
green	سَبز	sabz
groom (n.)	داماد	daamaad
ground	زَمین	zameen
group	گُروه	gorooh
growth	رُشد	roshd
guilt	گُناه	gonaah
guilty	گُناهکار	gonaahkaar
gum(s)	لَثه	lase
gun	تُفَنگ	tofang

H

had (he/she)	داشت	daasht
hail	تَگَرگ	tagarg
hair	مو	moo
halo	هاله	haale
hand	دَست	dast
handbag	کیف	keef
honeydew	خَربُزه	kharboze
happiness	خوشحالی، شادی	khoshhaalee
happy	خوشحال، شاد	khoshhaal
has (he/she)	دارَد	daarad
have (v.)	داشتَن	daashtan
hazelnut	فَندُق	fandogh
head	سَر	sar
health	سلامَت، سَلامتی	salaamat
healthy	سالم	saalem
heart	قَلب، دل	ghalb
heat	حَرارَت، گَرما	haraarat
heavy	سَنگین	sangeen
help (n.)	کُمَک	komak
help (v.)	کُمَک کَردَن	komak kardan
hence	بَنابَراین، در نَتیجه	banaa bar in
henna	حَنا	hanaa

English	Farsi	Transliteration
here	اینجا	eenjaa
Here you go!	بفَرمایید!	befarmaayeed
hero	قَهرِمان	ghahremaan
hi	سَلام	salaam
high school	دَبیرِستان	dabeerestaan
hijab (headdress)	حِجاب، چادُر، روسَری	hejaab
hips	باسَن	baasan
hire	اِستِخدام	estekhdaam
hire (v.)	اِستِخدام کَردَن	estekhdaam kardan
historian	تاریخ‌نگار، مُوَرِّخ	taarkh negaar
historical	تاریخی	taareekhee
history	تاریخ	taareekh
hit (v.)	زَدَن، زَد	zadan
hog	گُراز	goraaz
hole	سوراخ	sooraakh
home	خانه، مَنزِل	khaane
homosexual	هَمجِنسگِرا	hamjensgaraa
honest	راستگو	raastgoo
honey	عَسَل	asal
hookah	قَلیان	ghalyaan
hope	اُمید	omeed
hornet	زَنبور	zamboor
horse	اَسب	asb
horseback riding	اَسب سَواری	asb savaaree
hot	داغ	daagh
hour	ساعَت	saa'at
house	خانه	khaane
housing	مَسکَن	maskan
how	چطور، چِگونه	chetor
how many	چَند تا	chand taa
how much	چقَدر	cheghadr
human	اِنسان، آدَم	ensaan
human qualities	اِنسانیَّت	ensaneeyyat
humanities (minus arts)	عُلومِ اِنسانی	oloom e ensaanee
humid	مَرطوب	martoob
humiliated (adj.)	ذَلیل، تَحقیر شُده	zaleel
humiliation	ذِلَّت، تَحقیر	zellat

English	Farsi	Transliteration
husband	شوهَر	shohar
hygiene	بِهداشت	behdaasht

I

I	مَن	man
ice	یَخ	yakh
identical	یِکسان	yeksaan
idol	بُت	bot
if	اَگر، که، آیا	agar
Imam	اِمام	emaam
immediate	فوری	foree
implement (v.)	اِجرا کَردَن	ejraa kardan
imported	خارِجی، وارِداتی	khaarejee
impossible	غِیرِمُمکِن	gheyr e momken
in	تو، دَر	too
in other words	به عِبارتِ دیگر	be ebaarat e deegar
income	دَرآمَد	daraamad
income tax	مالیات بَر درآمد	maaleeyaat bar daraamad
incorrect	غَلَط، نادُرُست	ghalat
independence	اِستِقلال	esteghlaal
independent	مُستَقِل	mostaghel
individual	فَرد	fardaa
individuals	اَفراد	afraad
industrial	صَنعَتی	san'atee
industries	صَنایِع	sanaaye'
industry	صَنعَت	san'at
inform (v.)	اِطّلاع دادن	ettela' daadan
information	اِطّلاعات	ettela'aat
insect	حَشَره	hashare
insects	حَشَرات	hasharaat
inside	تو، داخِل	too
instruction	آموزش	aamoozesh
instructor	مُعَلِّم، اُستاد	mo'allem
intelligence	اِطّلاعات، هوش	ettela'aat
intelligent	باهوش	baahoosh
intention	قَصد	ghasd
intentionally	عَمداً	amdan

interest	سود، عَلاقه	sood
international	بینُالمِللی	byenolmelalee
intersection	تَقاطُع	taghaato'
interview	مُصاحِبه	mosaahebe
interview (v.)	مُصاحِبه کردن	mosaahebe kardan
intestine	روده	roode
interesting	جالِب	jaaleb
introduce (v.)	مُعَرّفی کردن	mo'arrefee kardan
introduction	مُعَرّفی	mo'arrefee
investigate (v.)	تَحقیق کردَن	tahgheeg kardan
investigation	تَحقیق	tahgheegh
Iran	ایران	eeraan
Iranian	ایرانی	eeraanee
Iraq	عَراق	araagh
is	اَست	ast
is not	نیست	neest
Islam	اِسلام	eslaam
issue	مُشکِل، مساله	moshkel
it means	یَعنی	ya'nee

J

jacket	کُت	kot
Jaleh (feminine name)	ژاله	zhaale
jam, jelly	مُرَبّا	morabbaa
Japan	ژاپُن	zhaapon
jar	شیشه	sheeshe
jasmine	یاس	yaas
jelly	ژِله	zhele
Judaism	یَهودیَت	yahoodeeyat
Jewish	کَلیمی، یَهودی	kaleemee
joint (adj.)	مُشتَرَک	moshtarak
journalist	خَبَرنگار	khabarnegaar
joy	لَذّت	lezzat
judge	قاضی	ghaazee
judge (v.)	قِضاوَت کردن	ghezaavat kardan

K

kabob	کَباب	kabaab

keyboard	کیبورد	keebord
Khordad (third month of the Persian calendar)	خُرداد	khordaad
kid	بَچّه	bachche
kilo	کیلو	keeloo
kind	مِهرَبان، نوع	mehrabaan
kindergarten	آمادِگی، پیشدَبِستانی	aamaadegee
kindness	مِهر	mehr
knee	زانو	zaanoo
knife	چاقو	chaaghoo
know	دانِستَن	daanestan
knowledge	دانِش	daanesh
Kuwait	کُویت	koveyt

L

lace	تور	toor
lack	عَدَم	adam
lady	خانُم، بانو	khaanom
lake	دَریاچه	daryaache
lamp	چِراغ	cheraagh
land	زَمین، خُشکی	zameen
lap	دور، روی پا	dor
laptop	لَپتاپ	laptaap
large	بُزُرگ	bozorg
last	آخَر، آخِرین	aakhar
last name	فامیلی، نام خانِوادگی	faameelee
last one	آخِرین	aakhareen
last year	پارسال	paarsaal
late	دیر، اَواخِر	deer
later	بَعداً	ba'dan
law	قانون، حُقوق	ghaanoon
leaf	بَرگ	barg
left	چَپ	chap
leftist	چَپگرا	chapgaraa
leg	پا، پایه	paaye
legible	خوانا	khaanaa
Leila (feminine name)	لِیلا	leylaa
leisure	تَفریح	tafreeh

English	Farsi	Transliteration
letter	نامه	naame
LGBTQIA+	دِگرباش	degarbaash
liar	دُروغگو	dorooghgoo
license plate	پلاک (ماشین)	pelaak
lie (n.)	دُروغ	doroogh
lie (v.)	دُروغ گُفتَن	doroogh goftan
life	زِندگی	zendegee
light	چِراغ، نور، روشَن	cheraagh
lightness	روشَنایی	roshanaayee
like	مانَند، مثل	maanand
like (v.)	دوست داشتَن، عَلاقه داشتَن	doost daashtan
limit	حُدود، حَد	hodood
line	صَف، خَط	saf
lion	شیر	sheer
liquid	مایِع	maaye'
little	کَم، کوچَک	kam
live (adj.)	زِنده	zende
load	بار	baar
local	مَحَلّی	mahallee
location, place	مَحَل	mahal
loneliness	تَنهایی	tanhaayee
look (v.)	نِگاه کَردَن	negaah kardan
loom	دار	daar
lose weight (v.)	لاغَر شُدَن، وَزن کَم کَردَن	laaghar shodan
loss	ضَرر، از دَست دادن	zarar
lots	بِسیار، زیاد	besyaar
love (n.)	مِهر، عِشق	mehr
low	کَم، پایین	kam
luck	شانس	shaans
lunch	ناهار	naahaar
lung(s)	ریه، شُش	reeye

M

maʾam	خانُم	khaanom
machine gun	مُسَلسَل	mosalsal
made	ساخت	saakht
mail (v.)	پُست کَردَن	post kardan
mailman	پُستچی	postchee
majority	اَکثَریَت	aksareeyat
make (v.)	دُرُست کَردَن	dorost kardan
make friends (v.)	دوست شُدَن	doost shodan
mal-	سوءِ، بَدِ	soo'
male	نَر	nar
mama	مامان	maamaan
man	اِنسان، مَرد	ensaan
management	مُدیریَت	modeereeyat
manager	مُدیر	modeer
manufacture (n.)	تولید	toleed
many	بِسیار، خِیلی، زیاد، چَندین	besyaar
Marine Corps	تُفنگداران دَریایی	tofangdaaraan e daryaayee
market	بازار	baazaar
married	مُتَأهّل	mote'ahhel
massage (n.)	ماساژ	maasaazh
massage (v.)	ماساژ دادَن	maasaazh daadan
master's degree	فوق لیسانس، کارشناسیِ ارشَد	fogh e leesaans
match	مُسابِقه، کِبریت	mosaabeghe
math	ریاضی	reeyaazee
matter	مادّه	maadde
maximum	حَداکثَر	hade'aksar
maybe	شایَد	shaayad
mayor	شَهردار	shahrdaar
me	مَن	man
meaning	مَعنی	ma'nee
meat	گوشت	goosht
medicine	دارو، دَوا	daaroo
meeting	جَلسه	jalase
Mehr (seventh month of the Persian calendar)	مِهر	mehr
member	عُضو	ozv
members	اَعضا	a'zaa
membership	عُضویَت	ozveeyat
memorize	حِفظ کَردَن	hefz kardan
menu	مِنو	meno

messy	كَثیف، نامُرَتَب	kaseef
middle	وَسَط	vasat
Middle East	خاوَرِ میانه	khaavar e meeyaane
military base	پادگان	paadegaan
milk	شیر	sheer
millennium	هِزاره	hezaare
million	میلیون	meelyoon
Mina (feminine name)	مینا	meenaa
minimum	حَداقَل	Hade'aghal
minority	اَقَلیّت	aghaleeyyat
minute	دقیقه	daghighe
Miriam (feminine name)	مَریَم	maryam
mirror	آینه	aayne
mis-	سوءـ، بَدـ	soo'
missing	گُم، گُم شُده	gom
mistake (n.)	اِشتِباه، خَطا	eshtebaah
mistake (v.)	اِشتِباه کَردَن	eshtebaah kardan
moist	مَرطوب	martoob
mom	مامان	maamaan
Monday	دوشَنبه	doshambe
money	پول	pool
monitor	مونیتور	moneetor
monkey	میمون	meymoon
month	ماه	maah
monthly	ماهانه	maahaane
mood	حال، مود	haal
moon	ماه	maah
Mordad (fifth month of the Persian calendar)	مُرداد	mordaad
morning	صُبح	sobh
mosque	مَسجِد	masjed
mosquito	پَشه	pashe
mother	مادَر	maadar
motor	موتور، ماشین	motor
motorcycle	موتورسیکلت، موتور	motorseeklet
mount	کوه	kooh

mouse	موش	moosh
moustache	سِبیل	sebeel
mouth	دَهان	dahaan
movement	حَرِکت	harekat
movie	فیلم	feelm
movie theatre	سینَما	seenamaa
Mr.	آقا	aagha
Ms.	خانُم	khaanom
mud	گِل	gel
mushroom	قارچ	ghaarch
music	موسیقی	mooseeghee
Muslim	مُسَلمان	mosalmaan
mute	لال	laal
mystery	راز	raaz

N

name	اِسم، نام	esm
naturally	طَبیعتاً	tabee'atan
nature	طَبیعَت	tabee'at
Navy	نیروی دَریایی	neeroo ye daryaayee
neck	گَردَن	gardan
nectarine	شَلیل	shaleel
need (n.)	اِحتیاج، نیاز	ehteeyaaj
need (v.)	اِحتیاج داشتَن	ehteeyaaj daashtan
needle	سوزَن	soozan
neighborhood	مَحَلّه	mahalle
network	شَبَکه	shabake
never	اَبداً، هَرگِز	abadan
new	جَدید، نو	jadeed
newborn	نوزاد	nozaad
news	اَخبار	akhbaar
next	بَعدی	ba'dee
niece/nephew (the child of one's brother)	بَرادَرزاده	baraadarzaade
niece/nephew (the child of one's sister)	خواهَرزاده	khaaharzaade
night	شَب	shab
nine	نُه	noh

English	Farsi	Transliteration
nine hundred	نُهصَد	nohsad
nineteen	نوزدَه	noozdah
ninety	نَوَد	navad
no	نَه، خِیر	na
no one	هیچ کَس	heech kas
noise	صِدا	sedaa
non-religious	غیرِمَذهَبی	gheyr e mazhabee
noon	ظُهر	zohr
north	شُمال	shomaal
northern	شُمالی	shomaalee
nose	بینی، دَماغ	beenee
notebook	دَفتَر	daftar
now	اَکنون	aknoon
number	شُماره، نُمره	shomaare
nurse (n.)	پَرَستار، نِرس	parastaar
nurse (v.)	پَرَستاری کَردَن، شیر دادَن	parastaaree kardan
nursing	پَرَستاری	parastaaree
nutrition	تَغذیه	taghzeeye
nutritious	مُغَذّی	moghazzee

O

obese	چاق	chaagh
obesity	چاقی	chaaghee
of	اَز	az
off	خاموش	khaamoosh
offer (n.)	پیشنَهاد	peeshnahaad
offer (v.)	عَرضه کَردَن، پیشنَهاد کَردَن	arze kardan
office	اِداره	edaare
office	دَفتَر، اِداره	daftar
offspring (no gender)	فَرزَند، بَچه	farzand
often	اَغلَب	aghlab
oil	روغَن، نَفت	roghan
old	بُزُرگ، پیر، مُسِن، قَدیمی، کُهنه	bozorg
on	رو(ی)، دَر	roo(ye)
one	یِک	yek
one hundred	صَد	sad
one thousand	هِزار	hezaar

English	Farsi	Transliteration
oneself	خود	khod
onion	پیاز	peeyaaz
only	فَقَط	faghat
opinion	نَظَر	nazar
or	یا	yaa
orange (adj.)	نارنجی	naarenjee
orange	پُرتُقال	portoghaal
order (n.)	نَظم، سِفارِش	nazm
Ordibehesht (second month of the Persian calendar)	اُردیبِهِشت	ordeebehesh
organization	سازمان	saazmaan
origin	اَصل	asl
original	اَصلی	aslee
originality	اِصالَت	esaalat
other	دیگَر	deegar
others	دیگَران	deegaraan
out	خارِج، بیرون	khaarej
oven	فِر	fer
over	رو(ی)، بالا(ی)	roo(ye)
owl	جُغد	joghd

P

pacifier	پِستانَک	pestaanak
page	صَفحه	safhe
pain	دَرد، تیر	dard
pain reliever	مُسَکِّن	mosakken
painful	دَردناک	dardnaak
paint (n.)	رَنگ	rang
paint (v.)	نَقّاشی کَردَن	naghghaashee kardan
painter	نَقّاش	naghghaash
painting	نَقّاشی	naghghashee
Pakistan	پاکِستان	paakestaan
palace	قَصر، کاخ	ghasr
panther	پَلَنگ	palang
parrot	طوطی	tootee
part	بَخش، قِسمَت	bakhsh
participate (v.)	شِرکَت کَردَن	mosharekat kardan

English	Farsi	Transliteration
participation	مُشارِکَت، شِرکَت	moshaarekat
parties (political)	أحزاب	ahzaab
party	حِزب، مِهمانی	hezb
pass (v.)	گُذَشتَن	gozashtan
passion	شور	shoor
past	گُذَشته	gozashte
paste	رُب، خَمیر	rob
path	مَسیر، راه	maseer
patient	بیمار، مَریض	beemaar
pay (v.)	پَرداخت کَردَن، پَرداختَن	pardaakht kardan
peace	صُلح، آرامِش	solh
peach	هُلو	holoo
pear	گُلابی	golaabee
pen (ball point)	خودکار	khodkaar
pencil	مِداد	medaad
pennyroyal	پونه	poone
people	مَردُم	mardom
pepper	فِلفِل	felfel
percent	دَرصَد	darsad
percentage	دَرصَد	darsad
period	دوره، دوران، مُدَّت	dore
Persian	فارسی، ایرانی	faarsee
person	نَفَر، فَرد، کَس	nafar
personal	خُصوصی	khosoosee
petroleum	نَفت	naft
physics	فیزیک	feezeek
physique	فیزیک،	feezeek
photographer	عَکّاس	akkaas
phrase	عِبارَت	ebaarat
phrases	عِبارات	ebaaraat
physician	پِزِشک، دُکتُر	pezeshk
pick up (v.)	بَرداشتَن	bardaashtan
pick up!	بَردار	bardaar
picked up	بَرداشت	bardaasht
pickpocket	جیب بُر	jeeb bor
pigeon	کَبوتَر	kabootar
pine	کاج	kaaj

English	Farsi	Transliteration
pineapple	آناناس	aanaanaas
pink	صورَتی	sooratee
pipe	پیپ	peep
pistol	هَفت‌تیر	hafteer
pitcher	پارچ	paarch
place	مَحَل، مَکان، جا	mahal
plain	دَشت	dasht
plan (n.)	بَرنامه	barnaame
plant	گیاه	geeyaah
plate	بُشقاب	boshghaab
play (n.)	بازی	baazee
please	لُطفاً	lotfan
pleasure	لِذَّت	lezzat
pocket	جیب	jeeb
point	نُقطه، نُکته	noghte
police	پُلیس	polees
policy	سیاسَت	seeyaasat
political	سیاسی	seeyaasee
politician	سیاسَتمَدار	seeyaasatmadaar
politics	سیاسَت	seeyaasat
pomegranate	أنار	anaar
port	بَندَر	bandar
portion	پُرس	pors
possible	مُمکِن	momken
Post Office	اداره‌ی پُست، پُستخانه	edaare ye post
potable	آشامیدَنی	aashaameedanee
potato	سیب‌زَمینی،	seebzameenee
power	قُدرَت	ghodrat
powerful	قُدرَتمَند	ghodratmand
prayer	دُعا	do'aa
precision	دِقَّت	deghghat
pregnant	باردار	baardaar
preparation	آمادِگی	aamaadegee
prepare (v.)	تَهیه کَردَن	taheeye kardan
presence	حُضور	hozoor
present	حاضِر، اَکنون، هِدیه	haazer
present (v.)	عَرضه کَردَن	arze kardan

English	Farsi	Transliteration
president	رَئیس‌جمهور	ra'ees jomhoor
press (n.)	مَطبوعات	matboo'aat
prevent (v.)	جلوگیری کَردَن	jelogeeree kardan
prime minister	نُخست‌وزیر	nokhost vazeer
principal	مُدیر	modeer
principle	أصل	asl
principles	أصول	osool
print (v.)	چاپ کَردَن	chaap kardan
printer	چاپگر	chaapgar
printing house	چاپخانه	chaapkhaane
private	خُصوصی، غیردولتی	khosoosee
problem	مُشکِل	moshkel
problems	مُشکِلات	moshkelaat
production	تولید	toleed
profit	سود	sood
program (n.)	بَرنامه	barnaame
promise (n.)	قول	ghol
promise (v.)	قول دادَن	ghol daadan
prosperous	آباد	aabaad
public	عُمومی،هَمگانی، دولَتی	omoomee
publish (v.)	مُنتَشر کَردَن	montasher kardan
publisher	اِنتِشارات	enteshaaraat
punishment	مُکافات، مُجازات	mokaafaat
pure	ناب	naab
puree	پوره	poore
purple	بَنفش	banafsh
purse	کیف	keef

Q

English	Farsi	Transliteration
Qatar	قَطَر	ghatar
quality	تَساوی	tasaavee
quiet (n.)	ساکِت	saaket

R

English	Farsi	Transliteration
rabbit	خَرگوش	khargoosh
race	نِژاد	nezhaad
racism	نِژادپَرستی	nezhaadparastee
racist	نِژادپَرست	nezhaadparast

English	Farsi	Transliteration
radio	رادیو	raadeeyo
railing	نَرده	narde
rain	باران	baaraan
rainy	بارانی	baaraanee
range	حُدود، بُرد	hodood
rare	نادِر	naader
ratify	تَصویب کَردَن	tasveeb kardan
raw	خام	khaam
read (past tense)	خواند	khaand
read (v.)	خواندَن	khaandan
readiness	آمادِگی	aamaadegee
ready	حاضِر، آماده	haazer
real	واقِعی	vaaghe'ee
reality	واقِعیَت	vaaghe'eeyat
really	واقِعاً	vaaghe'an
reason	دَلیل، عِلَّت	daleel
reasons	عِلَل، دَلایِل	elal
receipt (n.)	رسید	reseed
receive (v.)	دَریافت کَردَن، گِرفتَن	daryaaft kardan
received (v.)	گِرفت، دَریافت کرد	gereft
recreation	تَفریح	tafreeh
red	قِرمز	ghermez
regime, diet	رِژیم	rezheem
region	مَنطقه	mantaghe
regions	مَناطِق	manaategh
regulations	قوانین	ghavaaneen
related	مَربوط	marboot
relation	رابطه	raabete
relationship	رابطه	raabete
relatives	فامیل	faameel
religion	مَذهَب	mazhab
religious	مَذهَبی	mazhabee
repair	تَعمیر	ta'meer
report	گُزارش	gozaaresh
reporter	خَبَرنگار، گُزارشگَر	khabarnegaar
representative	نَماینده	namaayandeh
representatives	نَمایِندِگان	namaayandegaan

English	Farsi	Transliteration
republic	جُمهوری	jomhooree
Republican	جُمهوریخواه	jomhooreekhaah
request	خواهِش، دَرخواست	khaahesh
research (n.)	پِژوهِش، تَحقیق	pazhoohesh
research (v.)	تَحقیق کَردَن	tahgheeg kardan
researcher	پِژوهِشگر، مُحَقِّق	pazhooheshgar
respiration	تنفُّس	tanaffos
respond (v.)	پاسُخ دادَن، جَواب دادَن	paasokh daadan
response	پاسُخ، جَواب	paasokh
responsibility	مَسئولیَت	mas'ooleeyat
responsible	مَسئول	mas'ool
restaurant	رستوران	restooraan
result	نَتیجه	nateeje
revolution	اِنقلاب	enghalaab
Rial (Iranian currency)	ریال	reeyaal
rice	بِرنج	berenj
rice (cooked)	چُلو	cholo
ride (v.)	راندَن	raandan
right	راست، دُرُست، حَق	raast
rights	حقوق	hoghoogh
ring (n.)	حَلقه	halghe
river	رود	rood
road	جادّه	jaadde
room	اُتاق	otaagh
rooster	خُروس	khoroos
root	ریشه	reeshe
rope	طَناب	tanaab
rose water	گُلاب	golaab
round	گِرد	gerd
ruler	حاکِم، خَط کَش	haakem
rules	قَوانین	ghavaaneen
runner	دَوَنده	davande
Russia	روسیه	rooseeye

S

Saeed (masculine name)	سَعید	sa'eed
said	گُفت	goft
salad	سالاد	saalaad

English	Farsi	Transliteration
salary	حقوق	hoghoogh
sale	فُروش	foroosh
sales tax	مالیاتِ فروش	maaleeyaat e foroosh
salt	نَمَک	namak
salty	شور	shoor
Sarah	سارا	saaraa
sat	نِشَست	neshast
satin	ساتَن	saatan
Saturday	شَنبه	shambe
Saudi Arabia	عَرَبِستانِ سُعودی	arabestan e so'oodee
say (v.)	گُفتَن	goftan
schedule (n.)	بَرنامه	barnaame
school	مَدرسه	madrese
science	عِلم	elm
scream (n.)	جیغ	jeegh
scream (v.)	جیغ زَدَن	jeegh zadan
sea	دَریا	daryaa
seal	فُک	fok
season	فَصل	fasl
seaweed	جُلبَک	jolbak
second	دُوُّم	dovvom
second (time unit)	ثانیه	saaneeye
secret	راز، مَخفی	raaz
section	بَخش، قِسمَت	bakhsh
sector	بَخش	bakhsh
secular	سِکولار	sekoolaar
see (v.)	دیدَن	deedan
seed	بَذر	bazr
select (v.)	اِنتِخاب کردن	entekhaab kardan
send (v.)	فِرِستادَن	ferestaadan
sense	حِس	hes
sentence	جُمله	jomle
sentences	جُمَلات	jomalaat
seriously	جِدّاً	jeddan
services	خَدَمات	khadamaat
seven	هَفت	haft

English	Farsi	Transliteration
seven hundred	هَفتصَد	haftsad
seventeen	هِفدَه	hefdah
seventy	هَفتاد	haftaad
sewer	دوزَنده	doozande
shadow	سایه	saaye
shade	سایه	saaye
Shahrivar (sixth month of the Persian calendar)	شَهریوَر	shahreevar
shake (n.)	تِکان	tekaan
share	سَهم	sahm
share(s)	سَهام	sahaam
she/he/they	ایشان	eeshaan
she/he/they (singular)	او	oo
sheet	وَرَق	varagh
shellfish	صَدَف	sadaf
ship	کِشتی	keshtee
Shooshtar (city in Iran)	شوشتَر	shooshtar
shop (v.)	خَرید کَردَن	khareed kardan
shopping	خَرید	khareed
shore	ساحِل	saahel
should	باید	baayad
shout	داد	daad
show (n.)	بَرنامه	barnaame
sick	بیمار، مَریض	beemaar
sickle	داس	daas
sickness	بیماری، مَریضی	beemaaree
sign and seal	مُهر و موم	mohr o moom
silence	سُکوت	sokoot
silent	ساکِت	saaket
silver	نُقره	noghree
silver (adj.)	نُقره‌ای	nogree'ee
similar	شَبیه، مُشابه	shabih
simple	ساده	saade
sin	گُناه	gonaah
sinful	گُناهکار	gonaahkaar
single (person)	مُجَرَّد	mojarrad
Sir	آقا	aagha
sister	خواهَر	khaahar
sister-in-law (the wife of one's husband's brother)	جاری	jaaree
sister-in-law (wife of one's brother)	زَن بَرادَر	zan baraadar
sit (v.)	نِشَستَن	neshastan
six	شِش	shesh
six hundred	شِشصَد	sheshsad
sixteen	شانزدَه	shaanzdah
sixty	شَصت	shast
skin	پوست	poost
skirt	دامَن	daaman
sleep (n.)	خواب	khaab
sleep (v.)	خوابیدَن	khaabeedan
slippery	سُر	sor
small	کوچَک	koochak
smart	باهوش	baahoosh
smartphone	تِلِفُن هوشمَند	telefon e hooshmand
smoke (cigarettes) (v.)	سیگار کِشیدَن	seegaar kesheedan
smoke (hookah) (v.)	قَلیان کِشیدَن	ghalyaan kesheedan
snail	حَلَزون	halazoon
snow	بَرف	barf
snowy	بَرفی	barfee
so	پَس	pas
soap	صابون	saaboon
soccer	فوتبال	football
social	اِجتِماعی	ejtemaa'ee
society	جامِعه	jaame'e
sock(s)	جوراب	jooraab
soil	خاک	khaak
soldier	سَرباز	sarbaaz
solid (state of matter)	جامِد	jaamed
solution	مَحلول	mahlool
solve (v.)	حَل شُدَن	hal shodan
solvent	حَلّال	hallaal
some	بَرخی، بَعضی	barkhee
sometimes	گاهی	gaahee
son	پِسَر	pesar

son-in-law	داماد	daamaad		storm	طوفان	toofaan
song	آواز	aavaaz		story	داستان	daastaan
soon	زود	zood		straight	صاف	saaf
Soraya (feminine name)	ثُرَیّا	sorayyaa		straw	نی	ney
sound	صِدا، صوت	sedaa		street	خیابان	kheeyaabaan
soup	آش، سوپ	aash		strike (n.)	ضَربه، اِعتِصاب، حَمله	zarbe
sour	تُرش	torsh		student (college)	دانِشجو	daaneshjoo
source	منشأ	mansha'		student (K-12)	دانش آموز	daanesh aamooz
south	جُنوب	jonoob		study (v.)	دَرس خواندَن	dars khaandan
southern	جُنوبی	jonoobee		success	مُوَفَّقیَت	movaffagheeyat
space	فَضا	fazaa		successful	مُوَفَّق	movaffagh
special	مَخصوص، ویژه	makhsoos		such	چِنین	cheneen
Special Forces	نیروی ویژه	neeroo ye veezhe		sugar	شِکَر	shekar
specialist	مُتَخَصِّص	motekhasses		suggest (v.)	پیشنَهاد دادن، پیشنَهاد کَردَن	peeshnahaad daadan
specialty	تَخَصُّص	takhassos		suggestion	پیشنَهاد	peeshanhaad
spectator	تَماشاچی	tamashaachee		suitable	مُناسِب	monaaseb
spend (v.)	پَرداخت کردن، پَرداختَن	pardaakht kardan		suitcase	چَمدان	chamedaan
spicy	تُند	tond		sun	آفتاب	aaftaab
spider	عَنکَبوت	ankaboot		sun	خورشید	khorsheed
spoon	قاشُق	ghaashogh		Sunday	یکشَنبه	yekshambe
sport	وَرزِش	varzesh		sunglasses	عینک آفتابی	eynak aaftaabee
spouse	هَمسَر	hamsar		sunny	آفتابی	aaftaabee
square	میدان، مُرَبَع	meydaan		sunset	غُروب	ghoroob
stamp	مُهر، تَمبر	mohr		support	حِمایَت	hemaayat
stamp (v.)	مُهر زَدَن	mohr zadan		supporter	حامی، پُشتیبان	haamee
star	ستاره	setaare		sure	مُطمَئِن	motma'en
start (n.)	شُروع	shoroo'		surface	سَطح	sath
station	ایستگاه	eestgah		surname	نام خانوادگی	naam e khaanevaadegee
stem	ساقه	saaghe		Susa (ancient city in Iran)	شوش	shoosh
stew	خورِش	khoresh		swallow (bird)	پَرستو	parastoo
still	هَنوز، ساکِن	hanooz		sweet	شیرین	sheereen
stock	سَهام	sahaam		swing	تاب	taab
stock market	بازارِ بورس، بازارِ سَهام	bazaar e boors		sword	شَمشیر	shamsheer
stomach	معده	me'de		surfaces	سُطوح	sotooh
stone	سَنگ	sang		Syria	سوریه	sooreeye
Stop!	ایست!	eest				
store	اَنبار	ambaar				

T

table	میز	meez
tail	دُم	dom
take (v.)	بُردَن، گرِفتَن	bordan
talk (v.)	حَرف زَدَن	harf zadan
tangerine	نارِنگی	naarengee
tape	نَوار	navaar
tar	قیر	gheer
tasty	لَذیذ	lazeez
tax	مالیات	maaleeyaat
taxi	تاکسی	taaksee
tea	چای	chaay
teach	تَدریس کَردَن	tadrees kardan
teacher	مُعَلّم	mo'allem
teahouse (traditional)	قهوه‌خانه	ghahvekhane
team	تیم	teem
teapot	قوری	ghooree
tear (v.)	پاره کَردن	paare kardan
technical	فَنّی	fannee
technique	فَن	fan
Tehran	تِهران	tehraan
telephone	تِلِفُن	telefon
television	تِلِویزیون	televeezion
temple	مَعبَد	ma'bad
ten	دَه	dah
tent	چادُر	chaador
text message	اس ام اس، پیامَک	es em es
thankful	مَمنونِ، مُتشَکِر، سپاسگزار	mamnoon
thanks	مَمنون، مُتشَکِر، مِرسی	mamnoon
that	آن، که	aan
then	بَعد، سِپس	ba'd
there	آنجا	aanjaa
there is	هَست	hast
therefore	بَنابَراین	banaa bar in
these	اینها	eenhaa
they	آنها	aanhaa

thigh	ران	raan
thin	لاغر	laaghar
thing	چیز	cheez
think (v.)	فِکر کَردن	fekr kardan
third	سِوُّم	sevvom
thirteen	سیزدَه	seezdah
thirty	سی	see
this	این	een
thorn	خار	khaar
thought(s)	فِکر	fekr
three	سه	se
three hundred	سیصَد	seesad
Thursday	پَنجشَنبه	panjshambe
thus	بَنابَراین	banaa bar in
tiger	بَبر	babr
time	وَقت، زَمان، ساعَت	vaght
tip	اَنعام، نوک	an'aam
Tir (fourth month of the Persian calendar)	تیر	teer
title	عُنوان	onvaan
to	به	be
today	اِمروز	emrooz
toe	اَنگُشت، اَنگُشتِ پا	angosht
tomato	گوجه‌فَرَنگی	gojefarangee
ton	تُن	ton
tongue	زَبان	zabaan
too	هَم	ham
took	گِرِفت	gereft
Tooman (Iranian currency)	تومان	toomaan
tooth	دَندان	dandaan
top	بالا(ی)	baalaa
topic	موضوع	mozoo'
torn	پاره	paare
tornado	گِردباد	gerdbaad
tourism	جَهانگردی	jahaangardee
tourist	جَهانگرد	jahaangard
toward	سو(ی)	soo
train	قطار	ghataar

English	Farsi	Transliteration
translate	تَرجُمه کَردَن	tarjome kardan
translation	تَرجُمه	tajome
trap	دام	daam
travel (n.)	سَفَر	safar
travel (v.)	سَفَر رَفتَن، سَفَر کَردَن	safar raftan
travel across (v.)	طی کردن	tey kardan
tray	سینی	seenee
tree	دِرَخت	derakht
trial	مُحاکِمه	mohaakeme
triceps	بازو	baazoo
trouble (n.)	مُکافات، مُجازات	mokaafaat
true	صَحیح	saheeh
truth	راست، حَقیقَت	raast
try (v.)	سَعی کَردَن	sa'y kardan
tube	لوله	loole
Tuesday	سه‌شَنبه	seshambe
Turkey	تُرکیه	torkeeye
turn (n.)	نوبَت	nobat
turn on (v.)	روشَن کَردَن	roshan kardan
turn off (v.)	خاموش کَردَن	khaamoosh kardan
turquoise (adj.)	فیروزه‌ای	feerooze'ee
turquoise (n.)	فیروزه	feerooze
twelve	دَوازدَه	davaazdah
twenty	بیست	beest
two	دو	do
two hundred	دویست	deveest
type	نوع	no'
types	اَنواع	anzaa'

U

umbrella	چَتر	chatr
uncle (maternal)	دایی	daayee
uncle (paternal)	عَمو	amoo
under	زیر	zeer
unemployed	بیکار	beekaar
unequal	نابَرابر	naabaraabar
uniform	یونیفورم	yooneeform
unit	واحِد	vaahed

English	Farsi	Transliteration
united	مُتَّحِد	mottahed
United States	اَیالَاتِ مُتَّحِده، آمریکا	eeyaalaat e mottahede
unity	اِتّحاد	ettehaad
universe	جَهان	jahaan
university	دانشگاه	daaneshgaah
unwise	نادان	naadaan
up	بالا	baalaa
USA	آمریکا	aamreekaa
usually	مَعمولاً	ma'moolan

V

vegetable	سَبزی	sabzee
vegetarian	گیاهخوار	geeyaahkhaar
very	بِسیار، خِیلی	besyaar
victorious	پیروز	peerooz
victory	پیروزی	peeroozee
view	نَظَر، مَنظَره	nazar
village	روستا	roostaa
voice	صِدا	sedaa

W

wage	مُزد	mozd
waist	کَمَر	kamar
waiting (adj.)	مُنتَظِر	montazer
walk (v.)	راه رَفتَن	raah raftan
want (v.)	خواستَن	khaastan
warm	گَرم	garm
warrior	مُبارِز	mobaarez
was	بود	bood
watch (v.)	تَماشا کَردَن	tamaashaa kardan
water	آب	aab
watermelon	هِندِوانه	hendevaaneh
way	راه، مَسیر	raah
we	ما	maa
wealth	ثِرَوَت	servat
wealthy	ثِرَوَتمَند، دارا	servatmand
weather	هَوا	havaa
Wednesday	چَهارشَنبه	chaahaarshambe

week	هَفته	hafte	word	كَلمَه، واژه	kalame
weekly	هَفتگی	haftegee	words	كَلمات	kalamaat
weigh (v.)	وَزن كردَن	vazn kardan	work	كار	kaar
weight	وَزن	vazn	worker	كارگَر	kaaregar
Welcome!	خوش آمَدید!	khosh aamadeed!	world	جَهان، دُنیا	jahaan
were	بود، بودَند	bood	worldview	جَهانبینی	jahaanbeenee
west	غَرب	gharb	worm	كِرم	kerm
western	غَربی	gharbee	worse	بَدتَر	badtar
wet	تَر، خیس	tar	worst	بَدتَرین	badtareen
whale	نَهَنگ	nahang	wrist	مُچ	moch
what	چه چیز، چه	che cheez	write (v.)	نوشتَن	neveshtan
wheat	گَندُم	gandom	writer	نویسَنده	neveesande
when	وَقتی، كِی	vaght	writing (n.)	نوشته	neveshte
where	كُجا	kojaa	wrong	غَلَط، نادُرُست	ghalat
whether	آیا	aayaa	wrote	نِوِشت	nevesht
which	كُدام	kodaam		**Y**	
white	سِفید	sefeed			
whole	كامِل، كُل	kaamel	yard	حَیاط	hayaat
why	چِرا	cheraa	Yazd (city in Iran)	یَزد	yazd
widow	بیوه	beeve	year	سال	saal
win (n.)	بُرد	bord	yellow	زَرد	zard
win (v.)	بُردَن، بَرنده شُدَن	bordan	yes	آره، بَله	aare
wind	باد	baad	yesterday	دیروز	deerooz
window	شیشه، پَنجره	sheeshe	yet	هَنوز	hanooz
wine	شَراب	sharaab	yogurt	ماست	maast
wire	سیم	seem	you (singular/ plural)	تو، شُما	shomaa
wise	دانا	daanaa	You're welcome!	خواهِش می‌كنم!	khaahesh mikonam
with	با	baa			
without	بِدونِ، بی	bedoone	young	جَوان	javaan
wolf	گُرگ	gorg	youth	جَوانی	javaanee
woman	زَن	zan		**Z**	
won (v.)	بُرد	bord			
wood	چوب	choob	zero	صِفر	sefr

Farsi-English Dictionary

آ

آب	water	aab
آب و هَوا	climate	aab o havaa
آباد	prosperous	aabaad
آبان	8th month of the Persian calendar	aabaan
آبشُش	gill	aabshosh
آبی	blue	aabee
آتَش	fire	aatash
آتَش‌سوزی	fire	aatash soozee
آتَش‌نشانی	fire station	aatash neshaanee
آخَر	last, end	aakhar
آخِرین	last one	aakhareen
آدامس	chewing gum	aadaams
آذَر	9th month of the Persian calendar	aazar
آرامِش	peace, calm	aaraamesh
آرد	flour	aard
آره	yes	aare
آریا	masculine name	aareeyaa
آزاد	free	aazaad
آزادی	freedom	aazaadee
آزادیِ بَیان	freedom of speech	aazaadee ye bayaan
آژانس	agency	aazhaans
آسیا	Asia	aaseeyaa
آش	Persian traditional soup	aash
آشامیدَنی	potable	aashaameedanee
آغاز	beginning	aaghaaz
آفتاب	sun	aaftaab
آفتابی	sunny	aaftaabee
آفریقا	Africa	aafreeghaa
آفَرین	good job!	aafareen
آقا	Mr., sir, gentleman	aagha
آلمان	Germany	aalmaan
آمادِگی	readiness, preparation, kindergarten	aamaadegee

آمَد	(he/she) came	aamad
آمَدن	come (v.)	aamadan
آمریکا	America, USA	aamreekaa
آمریکایی	American	aamreekaayee
آموزِش	education, instruction	aamoozesh
آن	that	aan
آناناس	pineapple	aanaanaas
آنجا	there	aanjaa
آنها	they	aanhaa
آواز	song	aavaaz
آیا	whether, if	aayaa
آینده	future	aayande
آینه	mirror	aayne
اَبَداً	never	abadan
اَبر	cloud	abr
اَبری	cloudy	abree
اَبعاد	dimensions	ab'aad
اُتاق	room	otaagh
اِتّحاد	unity	ettehaad
اُتوبوس	bus	otoboos
اثاث	furniture	asaas
اَثَر	effect	asar
اِجتِماعی	social	ejtemaa'ee
اِجرا کَردَن	implement (v.)	ejraa kardan
اِحتیاج	need	ehteeyaaj
اَحزاب	parties (political)	ahzaab
اِحساس	feeling	ehsaas
اَخبار	news	akhbaar
اِداره	office	edaare
اداره‌یِ پُست	Post Office	Edaare ye post
اَرتِش	Army	artesh
اُردَک	duck	ordak
اُردیبِهِشت	2nd month of the Persian calendar	ordeebehesh
اُروپا	Europe	oroopaa

اَز	of, from	az
اس ام اس	text message	es em es
اَسب	horse	asb
اَسب سَواری	horseback riding	asb savaaree
اَست	is	ast
اُستاندار	governor	ostaandaar
اِستخدام	hire	estekhdaam
اِستخدام کَردَن	hire (v.)	estekhdaam kardan
اِستقلال	independence	esteghlaal
اِسفَند	12th month of the Persian calendar	esfand
اِسکِناس	banknote	eskenaas
اِسلام	Islam	eslaam
اِسم	name	esm
اِسم کوچَک	first name	esm e koochak
اِشتباه	mistake	eshtebaah
اِشتباه کَردَن	make a mistake (v.)	eshtebaah kardan
اِصالَت	originality, authenticity	esaalat
اَصل	origin	asl
اَصلی	original	aslee
اُصول	principles	osool
اُصولگرا	fundamentalist	osoolgaraa
اَصیل	authentic	aseel
اِضافه کَردَن	add (v.)	ezaafe kardan
اِضافی	extra	ezaafee
اِطّلاع دادن	inform (v.)	ettela' daadan
اِطّلاعات	information, intelligence	ettela'aat
اِطمینان	certainty	etmeenaan
اَعضا	members	a'zaa
اِعلام کَردَن	announce (v.)	e'laam kardan
اَغلَب	often	aghlab
اَفراد	individuals, persons	afraad
اَفغانِستان	Afghanistan	afghaanestaan
اِقتصاد	economy	eghtesaad
اَقلیّت	minority	aghaleeyyat
اَکثَریَت	majority	aksareeyat

اَکنون	now	aknoon
اَگَر	if	agar
اُلاغ	donkey	olaagh
اَلکُل	alcohol	alkol
اِلهام	Elham (feminine name)	elhaam
اَمّا	but	ammaa
اِمارات	Emirates (UAE)	emaaraat
اِمام	Imam	emaam
اِمروز	today	emrooz
اِمسال	current year	emsaal
اِمکانات	facilities, possibilities	emkaanaat
اُمید	hope	omeed
اَمیر	Ami (masculine name)	ameer
اَمین	Amin (masculine name)	ameen
اَنار	pomegranate	anaar
اَنبار	store	ambaar
اِنتخاب کَردَن	select (v.)	entekhaab kardan
اِنتخابات	elections	entekhaabaat
اِنتشارات	publisher	enteshaaraat
اَنجام دادَن	do (v.)	anjaam daadan
اِنِرژی	energy	enerzhee
اِنسان	human, man	ensaan
اِنسانیَّت	human qualities	ensaneeyyat
اَنعام	tip	an'aam
اِنقلاب	revolution	enghalaab
اَنگُشت	finger, toe	angosht
اِنگلیسی	English	engeleesee
اَنگور	grape(s)	angoor
اَنواع	types	anzaa'
او	she/he/they (singular)	oo
اَوَّل	first	avval
ایالات مُتَحِده	United States	eeyaalaat e mottahede
ایران	Iran	eeraan
ایرانی	Iranian	eeraanee
ایست	Stop!	eest
ایستگاه	station	eestgah

ایشان	she/he/they	eeshaan
ایمیل	email	eemeyl
این	this	een
اینجا	here	eenjaa
اینها	these	eenhaa

ب

با	with	baa
باب	door	baab
بابا	dad, daddy	baabaa
بابابُزُرگ	grandpa	baaba abozorg
باجناق	brother-in-law (a man's wife's sister's husband)	baajenaagh
باخُدا	godly	baakhodaa
باد	wind	baad
بادام	almond	baadaam
بار	load	baar
باران	rain	baaraan
بارانی	rainy	baaraanee
باردار	pregnant	baardaar
بارِک الله! (باریکلا)	Good job!	baareekallaa
بازار	market	baazaar
بازار آزاد	free market	bazaar e aazaad
بازارِ بورس	stock market	bazaar e boors
بازارِ سَهام	stock market	bazaar e sahaam
بازارِ سیاه	black market	bazaar e seeyaah
بازو	triceps	baazoo
بازی	game, play	baazee
باسَن	hips	baasan
باعث	cause	Baa'es
باغبان	gardener	baaghbaan
بالا(ی)	top, over	baalaa
بانک	bank	baank
باهوش	smart, intelligent	baahoosh
باید	should, have to, must	baayad
بَبر	tiger	babr
بُت	idol	bot

بَچه	child, kid	bachche
بُحران	crisis	bohraan
بُحرانی	critical	bohraanee
بَحرین	Bahrain	bahreyn
بَخش	section, part, sector	bakhsh
بَد	bad	bad
بَدتَر	worse	badtar
بَدتَرین	worst	badtareen
بَدَن	body	badan
بِدون	without	bedoone
بَذر	seed	bazr
بَرابَر	equal	baraabar
بَرابری	equality	baraabaree
بَرادَر	brother	baraadar
بَرادَرزاده	niece/nephew (the child of one's brother)	baraadarzaade
بَراَساس	based on, according to	bar asaas
بَرای	for	baraaye
بَرخی	some	barkhee
بُرد	win (n.), won (v.)	bord
بَردار	pick up!	bardaar
بَرداشت	picked up	bardaasht
بَرداشتَن	pick up (v.)	bardaashtan
بُردَن	take (v.), win (v.)	bordan
بَرف	snow	barf
بَرفی	snowy	barfee
بَرق	electricity	bargh
بَرگ	leaf	barg
بَرنامه	program (n.), show (n.), schedule (n.), plan (n.)	barnaame
بِرنج	rice	berenj
بَرنده شُدَن	win (v.)	barande shodan
بُزُرگ	large, big, old	bozorg
بِسیار	a lot, very, many	besyaar
بُشقاب	plate	boshghaab
بَعد	then	ba'd
بُعد	dimension	bo'd
بَعداً	later	ba'dan

بَعدی	next	ba'dee
بَعضی	some	ba'zee
بِفَرمایید!	Here you go!, go ahead!	befarmaayeed
بَله	yes	bale
بَنابَراین	therefore, thus, hence	banaa bar een
بَندَر	port	bandar
بنزین	gas (fuel)	benzeen
بَنَفش	purple	banafsh
به	to	be
به طورِ کُلّی	generally	be tore kollee
به عبارتِ دیگر	in other words	be ebaarat e deegar
به عَلاوه	additionally	be alaave
بِهتَر	better	behtar
بِهتَرین	best	behtareen
بهداشت	hygiene	behdaasht
بَهمَن	11th month of the Persian calendar	bahman
بوته	bush	boote
بود	was, were	bood
بودایی	Buddhist	boodaayee
بودجه	budget	boojje
بودَن	be (v.)	boodan
بودیسم	Buddhism	boodeesm
بور	blond	boor
بی	without	bee
بیابان	desert	beeyaabaan
بَیان کَردن	express (v.)	bayan kardan
بیست	20	beest
بیکار	unemployed	beekaar
بیمار	sick, patient	beemaar
بیماری	sickness, disease	beemaaree
بین	between	beyn
بینُالمِلَلی	international	Byenolmelalee
بینی	nose	beenee
بیوه	widow	beeve

پ

پا	leg + foot	paa
پادگان	military base	paadegaan
پارچ	pitcher	paarch
پارچه	fabric	paarche
پارسال	last year	paarsaal
پاره	torn	paare
پاره کَردن	tear (v.)	paare kardan
پاسُخ	response	paasokh
پاسُخ دادَن	respond (v.), answer (v.)	paasokh daadan
پاکت	envelope	paakat
پاکِستان	Pakistan	paakestaan
پانزدَه	15	paanzdah
پانصَد	500	paansad
پایان	end	paayaan
پایه	leg (of something like a chair)	paaye
پایین	down, bottom	paayeen
پَتو	blanket	patoo
پُخته	cooked	pokhte
پدَر	father	pedar
پِدَربُزُرگ	grandfather	pedarbozorg
پَر	feather	par
پُر	full	por
پُرتُقال	orange	portoghaal
پَرداخت کَردن	pay (v.), spend (v.), make a payment (v.)	pardaakht kardan
پَرداختَن	spend (v.), pay (v.)	pardaakhtan
پُرس	portion	pors
پَرَستار	nurse	parastaar
پَرَستاری	nursing	parastaaree
پَرَستو	swallow (bird)	parastoo
پَرَنده	bird	parande
پَرواز	flight	parvaaz
پَرواز کَردن	fly (v.)	parvaaz kardan
پَروانه	butterfly	parvaane
پِزشک	physician	pezeshk

پَژوهش	research	pazhoohesh
پَژوهشگر	researcher	pazhooheshgar
پَس	so	pas
پُست کَردن	mail (v.)	post kardan
پِستانَک	pacifier	pestaanak
پُستچی	mailman	postchee
پُستخانه	Post office	postkhaane
پِسَر	boy, son	pesar
پِسَرخاله	cousin (the son of one's maternal aunt)	pesar khaale
پِسَردایی	cousin (the son of one's maternal uncle)	pesar daayee
پِسَرعَمّه	cousin (the son of one's paternal aunt)	pesar amme
پِسَرعَمو	cousin (the son of one's paternal uncle)	pesar amoo
پُشت	back, behind	posht
پَشه	mosquito	pashe
پلاک (خانه)	house/apartment number	pelaak
پلاک (ماشین)	license plate	pelaak
پَلَنگ	panther	palang
پُلیس	police	polees
پَنج	5	panj
پَنجاه	50	panjaah
پَنجره	window	panjere
پَنجشَنبه	Thursday	panjshambe
پَنیر	cheese	paneer
پوره	puree	poore
پوست	skin	poost
پوشک	diaper	pooshak
پول	money	pool
پونه	pennyroyal	poone
پیاز	onion	peeyaaz
پَیامَک	text message	payaamak
پیر	old	peer
پیروز	victorious	peerooz
پیروز شُدَن	defeat (v.)	peerooz shodan
پیروزی	victory	peeroozee

پیش	before	peesh
پیشنَهاد	suggestion	peeshanhaad
پیشنَهاد دادن	suggest (v.)	peeshnahaad daadan
پیشنَهاد کردن	suggest (v.)	peeshnahaad kardan

ت

تا	by	taa
تأثیر	effect	ta'seer
تاب	swing	taab
تاج	crown	taaj
تاریخ	history, date	taareekh
تاریخنگار	historian	taarkh negaar
تاریخی	historical	taareekhee
تاریک	dark	taareek
تاریکی	darkness	taareekee
تازه	fresh, new	taaze
تاکسی	taxi	taaksee
تَب	fever	tab
تَبَر	ax	tabar
تَحقیق	research, investigation	tahgheegh
تَحقیق کَردن	conduct research, investigate	tahgheeg kardan
تَخَصُّص	specialty	takhassos
تَدریس کَردن	teach	tadrees kardan
تَر	wet	tar
تَرجُمه	translation	tajome
تَرجُمه کَردن	translate	tarjome kardan
تُرد	crispy	tord
تَرس	fear	tars
تُرش	sour	torsh
تُرکیه	Turkey	torkeeye
تَساوی	quality	tasaavee
تَشکیل دادَن	form (v.)	tashkeel daadan
تَصمیم	decision	tasmeem
تَصمیم گِرفتَن	decide	tasmeem gereftan
تَصویب کَردن	ratify	tasveeb kardan

تَعمیر	repair	ta'meer
تَغذیه	nutrition	taghzeeye
تَغییر	change	taghyeer
تَغییر دادَن	change something	taghyeer daadan
تَغییر کَردَن	change (v.)	taghyeer kardan
تَفاوُت	difference	tafaavot
تَفریح	leisure, recreation	tafreeh
تُفَنگ	gun	tofang
تُفنگداران دَریایی	Marine Corps	tofangdaaraan e daryaayee
تَقاطُع	intersection	taghaato'
تَقریباً	almost	taghreeban
تکان	shake, move	tekaan
تَکاوَر	commando	takaavar
تَگَرگ	hail	tagarg
تَلخ	bitter	talkh
تِلفُن	telephone	telefon
تِلفُن هَمراه	cell phone	telefon e hamraah
تِلفُن هوشمَند	smartphone	telefon e hooshmand
تِلویزیون	television	televeezion
تَماس	contact	tamaas
تَماشا کَردَن	watch (v.)	tamaashaa kardan
تَماشاچی	spectator	tamashaachee
تَمام	all, end	tamaam
تَمبِر	(postage) stamp	tamr
تَمیز	clean	tameez
تَن	body	tan
تُن	ton	ton
تُند	fast, spicy	tond
تنفُس	respiration	tanaffos
تَنها	alone	tanhaa
تَنهایی	loneliness	tanhaayee
تَنور	brick oven	tanoor
تهران	Tehran	tehraan
تَهیه کَردَن	prepare (v.)	taheeye kardan
تو	you, inside, in	to, too
تَوانِست	could, was able	tavaanest

تَوانِستَن	be able to	tavaanestan
تَوَجُّه	attention	tavajjoh
تور	lace	toor
تَوَسُّط	by	tavassot
توسی	gray	toosee
تَوَلُّد	birth, birthday	tavallod
تولید	production, manufacture	toleed
تومان	Tooman (Iranian currency)	toomaan
تیر	bullet, arrow, shot, sharp pain	teer
تیره	dark	teere
تیغ	blade	teegh
تیم	team	teem

ث

ثانیه	second (time unit)	saaneeye
ثَروَت	wealth	servat
ثَروَتمَند	wealthy	servatmand
ثُرَیّا	feminine name	sorayyaa

ج

جادّه	road	jaadde
جاذبه	gravity	jaazebe
جاری	current (adj.), sister-in-law (the wife of one's husband's brother)	jaaree
جالِب	interesting	jaaleb
جامِد	solid (state of matter)	jaamed
جامعه	society	Jaame'e
جِدّاً	seriously	jeddan
جَدید	new	jadeed
جَذّاب	attractive, appealing	jazzaab
جُرم	crime	jorm
جُزییات	details	joz'eeyyat
جَشنواره	festival	jashnvaare
جَعبه	box	ja'be
جُغد	owl	joghd
جُلبَک	seaweed, algae	jolbak

جَلَسه	meeting	jalase
جِلو	front	jelo
جِلوگیری کَردَن	prevent	jelogeeree kardan
جُمعه	Friday	jom'e
جُمَلات	sentences	jomalaat
جُمله	sentence	jomle
جُمهوری	republic	jomhooree
جُمهوریخواه	Republican	jomhooreekhaah
جَنگل	forest	jangal
جُنوب	south	jonoob
جُنوبی	southern	jonoobee
جَهان	world, universe	jahaan
جَهان	world	jahaan
جَهانبینی	worldview	jahaanbeenee
جَهانگرد	tourist	jahaangard
جَهانگردی	tourism	jahaangardee
جو	barley	jo
جَو	atmosphere	jav
جَواب	response	javaab
جَواب دادَن	respond, answer (v.)	javaab daadan
جَوان	young	javaan
جَوانی	youth	javaanee
جوجه	chick	jooje
جوراب	sock(s)	jooraab
جیب	pocket	jeeb
جیب‌بُر	pickpocket	jeebbor
جیغ	scream	jeegh
جیغ زَدَن	scream (v.)	jeegh zadan

چ

چاپ کَردَن	print (v.)	chaap kardan
چاپخانه	printing house	chaapkhaane
چاپگر	printer	chaapgar
چادُر	tent, long veil	chaador
چاق	fat, obese	chaagh
چاقو	knife	chaaghoo
چاقی	obesity	chaaghee

چای	tea	chaay
چَپ	left	chap
چَپگرا	leftist	chapgaraa
چَتر	umbrella	chatr
چِرا	why	cheraa
چِراغ	lamp, light	cheraagh
چَسب	glue	chasb
چِشم	eye	cheshm
چِطور	how	chetor
چِقَدر	how much	cheghadr
چِگونه	how	chegoone
چُلو	steamed rice	cholo
چَمدان	suitcase	chamedaan
چَند تا	how many	chand taa
چِنین	such	cheneen
چه چیز	what	che cheez
چَهار	4	chaahaar
چَهاردَه	14	chaahaardah
چَهارراه	four-way	chaahar rah
چَهارشَنبه	Wednesday	chaahaarshambe
چَهارصد	400	chaahaarsad
چِهِل	40	chehel
چوب	wood	choob
چون	because	chon
چیز	thing, stuff	cheez
چین	China	cheen
چینی	Chinese	cheenee

ح

حاضِر	present, ready	haazer
حاکِم	ruler	haakem
حال	now, mood	haal
حالا	now	haala
حامی	sponsor, supporter	haamee
حَتماً	certainly	hatman
حَتّی	even	hattaa
حَداَقَل	minimum, at least	hade'aghal

حَداَكثَر	maximum	hade'aksar
حُدود	limit, range	hodood
حَرارَت	heat	haraarat
حَرف زَدَن	talk (v.)	harf zadan
حَرکَت	movement	harekat
حَریق	fire	hareegh
حِزب	party (political)	hezb
حِس	sense	hes
حِساب	account, calculation	hesaab
حَشَرات	insects	hasharaat
حَشَره	insect	hashare
حُضور	presence	hozoor
حِفظ کَردَن	memorize	hefz kardan
حَق	right	hagh
حقوق	rights, law, salary	hoghoogh
حَقیقَت	truth	hagheeghat
حَل شُدَن	be dissolved, solve	hal shodan
حَل کردن	dissolve (v.)	hal kardan
حَلّال	solvent	hallaal
حَلَزون	snail	halazoon
حِمایَت	support	hemaayat
حَمل کَردَن	carry (v.)	haml kardan
حَنا	henna	hanaa
حوزه	field	hoze
حَیاط	yard	hayaat
حِیوان	animal	heyvaan

خ

خار	thorn	khaar
خارِج	out	khaarej
خارجی	foreign, imported	khaarejee
خاک	soil	khaak
خاکِستَر	ash	khaakestar
خاکِستَری	gray	khaakestaree
خاله	aunt (maternal)	khaale
خام	raw, crude	khaam
خامه	cream	khaame

خاموش	off	khaamoosh
خاموش کَردَن	turn off (v.)	khaamoosh kardan
خانُم	Ms., ma'am, lady	khaanom
خانه	house, home	khaane
خانواده	family	khaanevaade
خاوَرمیانه	Middle East	khaavar e meeyaane
خَبَرنگار	reporter, journalist	khabarnegaar
خُدا	god	khoda
خُداحافظ	goodbye	khodaahaafez
خُدانابٰاوَر	atheist	khodaanaabaavar
خدانابٰاوَری	atheism	khodaanaabaavaree
خَدَمات	services	khadamaat
خَراب	broken	khaaraab
خَربُزه	honeydew	kharboze
خَرچَنگ	crab	kharchang
خُرداد	3rd month of the Persian calendar	khordaad
خُردسال	child	khordsaal
خَرگوش	rabbit	khargoosh
خُروج	exit	khorooj
خُروجی	exit	khoroojee
خُروس	rooster	khoroos
خَرید	shopping	khareed
خَرید کَردَن	shop (v.)	khareed kardan
خَریدار	buyer	khareedaar
خَریدَن	buy (v.)	khareedan
خُشک	dry	khoshk
خُشکی	land	khoshkee
خُصوصی	personal, private	khosoosee
خَط کِش	ruler	khatkesh
خَطَر	danger	khatar
خَطَرناک	dangerous	khatarnaak
خَمیر	dough	khameer
خُنَک	cool	khonak
خواب	sleep (n.)	khaab
خوابیدَن	sleep (v.)	khaabeedan
خواستَن	want (v.)	khaastan

خوانا	legible	**khaanaa**
خواند	read (past tense)	**khaand**
خواندَن	read (v.)	**khaandan**
خواهَر	sister	**khaahar**
خواهَرزاده	niece/nephew (the child of one's sister)	**khaaharzaade**
خواهِش	request	**khaahesh**
خواهِش می‌کنم!	You're welcome!	**khaahesh mikonam!**
خوب	good	**khoob**
خود	oneself	**khod**
خودکار	pen (ball point)	**khodkaar**
خوردَن	eat (v.)	**khordan**
خورش	Persian stew	**khoresh**
خورشید	sun	**khorsheed**
خوش آمدید!	Welcome!	**khosh aamadeed!**
خوشحال	happy	**khoshhaal**
خوشحالی	happiness	**khoshhaalee**
خیابان	street	**kheeyaabaan**
خِیر	no, good (n.)	**kheyr**
خیس	wet	**khees**
خِیلی	very	**kheylee**

د

داخِلی	domestic, internal	**daakhelee**
داد	shout	**daad**
دادگاه	court	**daadgaah**
دادَن	give (v.)	**daadan**
دار	loom	**daar**
دارا	wealthy	**daaraa**
دارَد	(he/she) has	**daarad**
دارو	medicine	**daaroo**
داس	sickle	**daas**
داستان	story	**daastaan**
داستانی	fiction	**daastaanee**
داشت	(he/she) had	**daasht**
داشتَن	have (v.)	**daashtan**
داغ	hot	**daagh**
دام	trap	**daam**

داماد	groom, son-in-law	**daamaad**
دامَن	skirt	**daaman**
دانا	wise	**daanaa**
دانِستَن	know	**daanestan**
دانِش	knowledge	**daanesh**
دانِش آموز	student (K-12)	**daaneshaamooz**
دانِشجو	(college) student	**daaneshjoo**
دانِشگاه	university, college	**daaneshgaah**
دایماً	constantly	**daa'eman**
دایی	uncle (maternal)	**daayee**
دَبِستان	elementary school	**dabestaan**
دَبیرِستان	high school	**dabeerestaan**
دُختَر	girl, daughter	**dokhtar**
دُختَرخاله	cousin (the daughter of one's maternal aunt)	**dokhtar khaale**
دُختَردایی	cousin (the daughter of one's maternal uncle)	**dokhtar daayee**
دُختَرعَمّه	cousin (the daughter of one's paternal aunt)	**dokhtar amme**
دُختَرعَمو	cousin (the daughter of one's paternal uncle)	**dokhtar amoo**
دَر	door, in	**dar**
دَرآمد	income	**daraamad**
دَربار	court	**darbaar**
دَرباره	about	**darbaare**
دَربان	doorkeeper	**darbaan**
دِرَخت	tree	**derakht**
دَرد	pain	**dard**
دَردناک	painful	**dardnaak**
دَرس خواندَن	study (v.)	**dars khaandan**
دُرُست	correct, right	**dorost**
دُرُست کَردَن	fix (v.), make (v.)	**dorost kardan**
دَرصَد	percent, percentage	**darsad**
دَروازه	gate	**darvaaze**
دُروغ	lie	**doroogh**
دُروغ گُفتَن	lie (v.)	**doroogh goftan**
دُروغگو	liar	**dorooghgoo**
دَریا	sea	**daryaa**
دَریاچه	lake	**daryaache**

دَریافت کَردَن	receive (v.)	**daryaaft kardan**
دَست	arm + hand	**dast**
دَستگاه	device	**dastgaah**
دَشت	plain	**dasht**
دُعا	prayer	**do'aa**
دِفاع	defense	**defaa'**
دَفتَر	office, notebook	**daftar**
دِقّت	precision	**deghghat**
دقیقه	minute	**daghighe**
دُکتُر	doctor	**doktor**
دکترا	doctorate	**doktoraa**
دِگَرباش	LGBTQIA+	**degarbaash**
دُلار	dollar	**dolaar**
دَلیل	reason	**daleel**
دُم	tail	**dom**
دَماغ	nose	**damaagh**
دموکرات	democrat	**demokraat**
دموکراسی	democracy	**demokraasee**
دَندان	tooth	**dandaan**
دُنیا	world	**donyaa**
دَه	10	**dah**
دَهان	mouth	**dahaan**
دهه	decade	**dahe**
دو	2	**do**
دَوا	medicine	**davaa**
دَوازدَه	12	**davaazdah**
دوچَرخه	bicycle	**docharkhe**
دوچَرخه سَواری کَردَن	cycle (v.)	**dochrkhe savaaree kardan**
دور	lap, far	**dor, door**
دوران	era	**doraan**
دورنگار	fax	**doornegaar**
دوره	period	**dore**
دوزَنده	sewer	**doozande**
دوست	friend	**doost**
دوست داشتَن	like (v.)	**doost daashtan**
دوست شُدَن	make friends (v.)	**doost shodan**

دوستپِسَر	boyfriend	**doost pesar**
دوستدُختَر	girlfriend	**doost dokhtar**
دوستی	friendship	**doostee**
دوشَنبه	Monday	**doshambe**
دوغ	Persian yoghurt drink	**doogh**
دولَت	government	**dolat**
دولَتی	public, run by the government	**dolatee**
دُوُم	second	**dovvom**
دَونده	runner	**davande**
دویست	200	**deveest**
دی	10th month of the Persian calendar	**dey**
دیپلُم	diploma	**deeplom**
دیدَن	see (v.)	**deedan**
دیر	late	**deer**
دیروز	yesterday	**deerooz**
دیگر	other	**deegar**
دیگران	others	**deegaraan**

ذ

ذُرَّت	corn	**zorrat**
ذِلَّت	humiliation	**zellat**
ذَلیل	humiliated (adj.)	**zaleel**

ر

رئیس	director, boss	**ra'ees**
رَئیسجمهور	president	**ra'ees jomhoor**
رابِطه	relation, relationship	**raabete**
رادیو	radio	**raadeeyo**
راز	mystery, secret	**raaz**
راستِ	right, truth	**raast**
راستگرا	conservative (politics)	**raastgaraa**
راستگو	honest	**raastgoo**
ران	thigh	**raan**
راندَن	ride (v.)	**raandan**
رانندگی کَردَن	drive (v.)	**raanandegee kardan**
رانَنده	driver	**raanande**

راه	path, way	**raah**
راه رَفتَن	walk (v.)	**raah raftan**
رایانه	computer	**raayaane**
رُب	thickened sauce	**rob**
رژیم	regime, diet	**rezheem**
رژیم گرفتَن	diet (v.)	**rezheem gereftan**
رستوران	restaurant	**restooraan**
رسید	receipt (n.)	**reseed**
رُشد	growth	**roshd**
رِفاقَت	friendship	**refaaghat**
رَفتَن	go (v.)	**raftan**
رَفیق	friend	**rafeegh**
رَنگ	color, paint	**rang**
رو(ی)	on, over	**roo(ye)**
رَوابِط	relationship	**ravaabet**
روبرو	facing	**rooberoo**
رود	river	**rood**
روده	intestine	**roode**
روز	day	**rooz**
روستا	village	**roostaa**
روسیه	Russia	**rooseeye**
روشَن	light, bright	**roshan**
روشَنایی	lightness	**roshanaayee**
روغَن	oil	**roghan**
ریاضی	math	**reeyaazee**
ریال	Rial (Iranian currency)	**reeyaal**
ریش	beard	**reesh**
ریشه	root	**reeshe**
ریه	lung(s)	**reeye**

ز

زانو	knee	**zaanoo**
زَبان	tongue	**zabaan**
زِبر	coarse	**zebr**
زَد	hit (past tense), applied	**zad**
زَدَن	hit (v.), apply (v.)	**zadan**
زَر	gold	**zar**

زَرّافه	giraffe	**zarraafe**
زَرد	yellow	**zard**
زَمان	time, period	**zamaan**
زَمین	ground, land, earth	**zameen**
زَن	woman, female	**zan**
زَن بَرادَر	sister-in-law (wife of one's brother)	**zan baraadar**
زَنبور	bee, hornet	**zamboor**
زِندِگی	life	**zendegee**
زِنده	live (adj.)	**zende**
زَنگ	bell	**zang**
زَنگ زَدَن	ring (v.), call (v.)	**zang zadan**
زود	early, soon	**zood**
زیاد	lots	**zeeyaad**
زیرِ	under, beneath	**zeer**
زیره	cumin	**zeere**
زیست شِناسی	biology	**zeest shenaasee**

ژ

ژاپُن	Japan	**zhaapon**
ژاکِت	cardigan	**zhaket**
ژاله	feminine name	**zhaale**
ژِله	jello, jelly	**zhele**

س

ساتَن	satin	**saatan**
ساحِل	shore, beach	**saahel**
ساخت	made	**saakht**
ساختَن	make (v.), build (v.)	**saakhtan**
ساده	simple, easy	**saade**
سارا	Sarah	**saaraa**
سازمان	organization	**saazmaan**
ساعَت	hour, clock	**saa'at**
ساقه	stem	**saaghe**
ساکِت	quiet, silent	**saaket**
سال	year	**saal**
سالاد	salad	**saalaad**
سالانه	annual	**saalaane**

سالِم	healthy	**saalem**
سایه	shade, shadow	**saaye**
سَبَد	basket	**sabad**
سَبز	green	**sabz**
سَبزی	vegetable	**sabzee**
سِبیل	moustache	**sebeel**
سِپَس	then	**sepas**
سِتاره	star	**setaare**
سَده	century	**sade**
سَر	head	**sar**
سُر	slippery	**sor**
سَرباز	soldier	**sarbaaz**
سَرد	cold (adj.)	**sard**
سَرما	cold (n.)	**sarmaa**
سَطح	surface	**sath**
سَطل	bucket	**satl**
سُطوح	surfaces	**sotooh**
سَعی کَردَن	try (v.)	**sa'y kardan**
سَعید	masculine name	**sa'eed**
سَفَر	trip, travel	**safar**
سَفَر رَفتَن	travel (v.), go on a trip	**safar raftan**
سَفَر کَردَن	travel (v.), go on a trip	**safar kardan**
سفید	white	**sefeed**
سِکّه	coin	**sekke**
سُکوت	silence	**sokoot**
سِکولار	secular	**sekoolaar**
سَگ	dog	**sag**
سَلام	hi	**salaam**
سَلامَت	health	**salaamat**
سَلامتی	health	**salaamatee**
سَنگ	stone	**sang**
سَنگین	heavy	**sangeen**
سه	3	**se**
سِهام	share(s), stock	**sahaam**
سه‌شَنبه	Tuesday	**seshambe**
سَهم	share	**sahm**
سو(ی)	toward	**soo**

سوء	mis-, mal-	**soo'**
سوپ	soup	**soop**
سود	interest, benefit, profit	**sood**
سوراخ	hole	**sooraakh**
سوریه	Syria	**sooreeye**
سوزَن	needle	**soozan**
سوسک	beetle, cockroach	**soosk**
سِوُّم	third	**sevvom**
سی	30	**see**
سیاسَت	policy, politics	**seeyaasat**
سیاسَتمَدار	politician	**seeyaasatmadaar**
سیاسی	political	**seeyaasee**
سیاه	black	**seeyaah**
سیب	apple	**seeb**
سیب‌زَمینی	potato	**seebzameenee**
سیر	garlic	**seer**
سیزدَه	13	**seezdah**
سیصَد	300	**seesad**
سیگار	cigarette	**seegaar**
سیگارکشیدَن	smoke (cigarettes) (v.)	**seegaar kesheedan**
سیگاربَرگ	cigar	**seegaarbarg**
سِیل	flood	**seyl**
سیم	cable, wire	**seem**
سینَما	movie theatre, cinema	**seenamaa**
سینی	tray	**seenee**

ش

شاد	happy	**shaad**
شام	dinner	**shaam**
شانزدَه	16	**shaanzdah**
شانس	luck	**shaans**
شانه	comb	**shaane**
شایَد	maybe	**shaayad**
شَب	night	**shab**
شَبَکه	network	**shabake**
شَبیه	similar	**shabih**
شُتُر	camel	**shotor**

شُد	became	**shod**
شُدَن	become (v.)	**shodan**
شَراب	wine	**sharaab**
شَرابی	burgundy (adj.)	**sharaabee**
شَرط	condition	**shart**
شَرق	east	**shargh**
شَرقی	eastern	**sharghee**
شِرکَت	participation, company	**sherkat**
شُروط	conditions	**shoroot**
شُروع	start, beginning	**shoroo'**
شُش	lung(s)	**shosh**
شِش	6	**shesh**
شِشصَد	600	**sheshsad**
شَصت	60	**shast**
شِکَر	sugar	**shekar**
شِکَست	defeat (n.)	**shekast**
شِکَست دادَن	defeat (v.)	**shekast daadan**
شِکَستَن	break (v.)	**shekastan**
شِکل	form (n.)	**shekl**
شِکَم	belly	**shekam**
شَلیل	nectarine	**shaleel**
شُما	you (singular and plural)	**shomaa**
شُمارِش	the act of counting	**shomaaresh**
شُمارِه	number	**shomaare**
شُمال	north	**shomaal**
شُمالی	northern	**shomaalee**
شُمُردَن	count (v.)	**shemordan**
شَمشیر	sword	**shamsheer**
شَنبه	Saturday	**shambe**
شَهر	city	**shahr**
شَهردار	mayor	**shahrdaar**
شَهریوَر	6th month of the Persian calendar	**shahreevar**
شور	salty, passion	**shoor**
شوش	ancient city in Iran	**shoosh**
شوشتَر	city in Iran	**shooshtar**
شوهَر	husband	**shohar**

شوهَرخواهَر	brother-in-law (one's sister's husband)	**shohar khale**
شیر	milk, lion, faucet	**sheer**
شیرخُشک	(baby) formula	**sheer e khoshk**
شیرین	sweet	**sheereen**
شیشه	glass, window, jar	**sheeshe**
شیمی	chemistry (science)	**sheemee**

ص

صابون	soap	**saaboon**
صاف	straight, flat	**saaf**
صُبح	morning	**sobh**
صُبحانه	breakfast	**sobhaane**
صَحرا	desert	**sahraa**
صَحیح	correct, true	**saheeh**
صَد	100	**sad**
صِدا	sound, noise, voice	**sedaa**
صَدَف	shellfish	**sadaf**
صَف	line	**saf**
صَفحه	page	**safhe**
صِفر	zero	**sefr**
صُلح	peace	**solh**
صَلیب	cross (n.)	**saleeb**
صَنایع	industries	**sanaaye'**
صَندَلی	chair	**sandalee**
صَنعَت	industry	**san'at**
صَنعَتی	industrial	**san'atee**
صورَت	face	**soorat**
صورَتحِساب	bill, check	**soorathesaab**
صورَتی	pink	**sooratee**

ض

ضَربه	strike (n.)	**zarbe**
ضَرر	loss, damage	**zarar**

ط

طالِبی	cantaloupe	**taalebee**
طَبیعَت	nature	**tabee'at**
طَبیعَتاً	naturally	**tabee'atan**

طَلا	gold	**talaa**
طَلایی	golden	**talayee**
طَناب	rope	**tanaab**
طوطی	parrot	**tootee**
طوفان	storm	**toofaan**
طِی	during	**tey**
طِی کردن	travel across (v.)	**tey kardan**

ظ

ظَرف	container, dish(es)	**zarf**
ظُهر	noon	**zohr**

ع

عاشِق شُدَن	fall in love (v.)	**aashegh shodan**
عِبارات	phrases	**ebaaraat**
عِبارَت	phrase	**ebaarat**
عَدَم	lack	**adam**
عَراق	Iraq	**araagh**
عَرَبِستان سُعودی	Saudi Arabia	**arabestan e so'oodee**
عَرضه کردن	present (v.), offer (v.)	**arze kardan**
عَروس	bride	**aroos**
عَسَل	honey	**asal**
عشق	love (n.)	**eshgh**
عَصر	evening, era	**asr**
عُضو	member	**ozv**
عُضوِیَت	membership	**ozveeyat**
عَکّاس	photographer	**akkaas**
عَلاقه	interest	**alaaghe**
عَلاقه داشتَن	like (v.), be interested (v.)	**alaaghe daashtan**
عِلَّت	reason	**ellat**
عِلَل	reasons	**elal**
عِلم	science	**elm**
عُلومِ اِنسانی	humanities (minus arts)	**oloom e ensaanee**
عَلی	Ali (masculine name)	**alee**
عَلیرَغم	despite	**alaa raghm**
عَمداً	intentionally	**amdan**

عَمّه	aunt (paternal)	**amme**
عَمو	uncle (paternal)	**amoo**
عُمومی	public	**omoomee**
عَنکَبوت	spider	**ankaboot**
عُنوان	title	**onvaan**
عِینَک	eyeglasses	**eynak**
عِینک آفتابی	sunglasses	**eynak aaftaabee**

غ

غایِب	absent	**ghaayeb**
غَذا	food	**ghazaa**
غَرب	west	**gharb**
غَربی	western	**gharbee**
غُروب	sunset	**ghoroob**
غَلَط	wrong, incorrect	**ghalat**
غُنچه	bud (flower)	**ghonche**
غِیبَت	absence, gossip	**gheybat**
غِیبَت کردَن	be absent, gossip (v.)	**gheybat kardan**
غِیرمَذهَبی	non-religious	**gheyr e mazhabee**
غِیرمُمکِن	impossible	**gheyr e momken**

ف

فارسی	Farsi, Persian	**faarsee**
فاکس	fax	**faaks**
فالوده	Persian dessert	**faaloode**
فامیل	relatives	**faameel**
فامیلی	last name	**faameelee**
فِر	curly, oven	**fer**
فَرانسه	France	**faraanse**
فَرد	individual	**fardaa**
فَرزَند	offspring, one's child (no gender)	**farzand**
فِرِستادَن	send (v.)	**ferestaadan**
فَرهَنگ	culture	**farhang**
فَرهَنگی	cultural	**farhangee**
فُرودگاه	airport	**foroodgaah**
فَروَردین	1st month of the Persian calendar	**farvardeen**
فُروش	sale	**foroosh**

فَرید	masculine name	**fareed**
فِستیوال	festival	**festeevaal**
فَصل	season	**fasl**
فَضا	space	**fazaa**
فَقَط	only, just	**faghat**
فِکر	thought(s)	**fekr**
فِکر کَردَن	think (v.)	**fekr kardan**
فِلفِل	pepper	**felfel**
فَن	technique	**fan**
فَندُق	hazelnut	**fandogh**
فَنّی	technical	**fannee**
فوتبال	soccer	**football**
فوتبالِ آمریکایی	football	**football aamreekaayee**
فوری	immediate	**foree**
فوقِ دیپلُم	associate degree	**fogh e deeplom**
فوقِ لیسانس	master's degree	**fogh e leesaans**
فیروزه	turquoise (n.)	**feerooze**
فیروزه‌ای	turquoise (adj.)	**feerooze'ee**
فیزیک	physics, physique	**feezeek**
فیل	elephant	**feel**
فیلم	movie, film	**feelm**

ق

قارچ	mushroom, fungus	**ghaarch**
قاشُق	spoon	**ghaashogh**
قاضی	judge	**ghaazee**
قانون	law	**ghaanoon**
قانونِ اَساسی	Constitution	**ghanoon e asaasee**
قایق	boat	**ghaayegh**
قَبل	before	**ghabl**
قَبلاً	before	**ghablan**
قُدرَت	power	**ghodrat**
قُدرَتمَند	powerful	**ghodratmand**
قَدیمی	old	**ghadeemee**
قَرار	appointment, date	**gharaar**
قِرمِز	red	**ghermez**
قَرن	century	**gharn**

قَصد	intention	**ghasd**
قَصر	palace	**ghasr**
قضاوَت کردن	judge (v.)	**ghezaavat kardan**
قَطار	train	**ghataar**
قَطَر	Qatar	**ghatar**
قَطره	drop	**ghatre**
قَطع کَردن	cut (v.)	**ghat' kardan**
قَفَس	cage	**ghafas**
قَلب	heart	**ghalb**
قَلعه	castle	**ghal'e**
قَلیان	hookah, shisha	**ghalyaan**
قَلیان کِشیدَن	smoke (hookah) (v.)	**ghalyaan kesheedan**
قَناری	canary	**ghanaaree**
قَهرِمان	champion, hero	**ghahremaan**
قَهرِمانی	championship	**ghahremaanee**
قَهوه	coffee	**ghahve**
قَهوه‌ای	brown	**ghahve'ee**
قهوه‌خانه	(traditional) teahouse	**ghahvekhane**
قَوانین	rules and regulations	**ghavaaneen**
قوری	teapot	**ghooree**
قول	promise (n.)	**ghol**
قیر	tar	**gheer**

ک

کاج	pine	**kaaj**
کاخ	palace	**kaakh**
کار	work	**kaar**
کاردانی	associate degree	**kaardaanee**
کارشِناس	expert	**kaarshenaas**
کارشِناسی	bachelor's degree	**kaarshenaasee**
کارشِناسی اَرشد	master's degree	**kaarshenaasee e arshad**
کارگَر	worker	**kaaregar**
کارمَند	clerk	**kaarmand**
کاسه	bowl	**kaase**
کافی‌شاپ	coffee shop	**kaafeeshaap**
کامپیوتر	computer	**kaampeeyooter**

کاملاً	completely	**kaamelan**
کانادا	Canada	**kaanaadaa**
کباب	kabob	**kabaab**
کبوتَر	pigeon	**kabootar**
کبود	bruise	**kabood**
کتاب	book	**ketaab**
کَثیف	dirty, messy	**kaseef**
کُجا	where	**kojaa**
کُدام	which	**kodaam**
کَرد	did	**kard**
کَردَن	do (v.)	**kardan**
کِرم	worm	**kerm**
کَره	butter	**kare**
کشاوَرز	farmer	**keshaavarz**
کِشتی	ship	**keshtee**
کِشوَر	country	**keshvar**
کَف	foam	**kaf**
کُل	all, entire	**kol**
کلاس	class	**kelaas**
کَلاغ	crow	**kalaagh**
کَلَمات	words	**kalamaat**
کَلَمه	word	**kalame**
کَلیمی	Jewish	**kaleemee**
کَم	low, little	**kam**
کَمَر	waist, lower back	**kamar**
کُمَک	help (n.)	**komak**
کُمَک کَردَن	help (v.)	**komak kardan**
کُمیته	committee	**komeete**
کُنتُرل کَردَن	control (v.)	**kontorol kardan**
که	that, if	**ke**
کُهنه	old	**kohne**
کوچَک	small	**koochak**
کوچه	alley	**kooche**
کودَک	child	**koodak**
کودَکِستان	day care center	**koodakestaan**
کولاک	blizzard	**koolaak**
کوه	mount	**kooh**

کُویت	Kuwait	**koveyt**
کِی	when	**key**
کیبورد	keyboard	**keebord**
کیف	handbag, purse	**keef**
کیلو	kilo	**keeloo**

گ

گاراژ	garage	**gaaraazh**
گاز	gas (state of matter)	**gaaz**
گاهی	sometimes	**gaahee**
گُذَشتَن	pass (v.), cross (v.), forgive (v.)	**gozashtan**
گُذَشته	past	**gozashte**
گُراز	hog	**goraaz**
گُربه	cat	**gorbe**
گِرد	round	**gerd**
گِردباد	tornado	**gerdbaad**
گَردَن	neck	**gardan**
گِرفت	took, received (v.)	**gereft**
گِرفتَن	take, receive (v.)	**gereftan**
گُرگ	wolf	**gorg**
گَرم	warm	**garm**
گَرما	heat	**garma**
گُروه	group	**gorooh**
گُزارِش	report	**gozaaresh**
گُسترِش	expansion	**gostaresh**
گُفت	said	**goft**
گُفتَن	say (v.)	**goftan**
گُل	flower	**gol**
گِل	mud	**gel**
گُلاب	rose water	**golaab**
گُلابی	pear	**golaabee**
گُم	missing	**gom**
گُناه	guilt, sin	**gonaah**
گُناهکار	guilty, sinful	**gonaahkaar**
گَندُم	wheat	**gandom**
گوجهفَرَنگی	tomato	**gojefarangee**
گوش	ear	**goosh**

گوشت	meat	**goosht**
گوشتخوار	carnivore	**gooshtkhaar**
گیاه	plant	**geeyaah**
گیاهخوار	vegetarian	**geeyaahkhaar**
گیلاس	cherry	**geelaas**

ل

لاغر	thin	**laaghar**
لاغر شُدَن	lose weight (v.)	**laaghar shodan**
لال	mute	**laal**
لباس	clothing	**lebaas**
لَپتاپ	laptop	**laptaap**
لَثه	gum(s)	**lase**
لَذَّت	joy, pleasure	**lezzat**
لَذیذ	delicious, tasty	**lazeez**
لُطفاً	please	**lotfan**
الله	god (in Arabic)	**allaah**
لوله	tube, pipe	**loole**
لیسانس	bachelor's degree	**leesaans**
لیلا	feminine name	**leylaa**
لیوان	cup, glass	**leevaan**

م

ما	we	**maa**
مأمورِ آتش‌نشانی	fire fighter	**ma'moor e atashneshaanee**
مُؤَثِّر	effective	**mo'asser**
مادَر	mother	**maadar**
مادَربُزُرگ	grandmother	**maadar bozorg**
مادّه	matter, female	**maadde**
ماساژ	massage	**maasaazh**
ماساژ دادَن	massage (v.)	**maasaazh daadan**
ماست	yogurt	**maast**
ماشین	car, engine	**maasheen**
مالی	financial	**maalee**
مالیات	tax	**maaleeyaat**
مالیات بر درآمد	income tax	**maaleeyaat bar daraamad**
مالیاتِ فروش	sales tax	**maaleeyaat e foroosh**
مامان	mama, mom	**maamaan**
مامان‌بُزُرگ	grandma	**maamaan bozorg**
مانَند	like	**maanand**
مانیتور	monitor	**moneetor**
ماه	moon, month	**maah**
ماهانه	monthly	**maahaane**
ماهی	fish	**maahee**
مایِع	liquid	**maaye'**
مُبارِز	warrior	**mobaarez**
مُبارِزه	fight	**mobaareze**
مُبارِزه کَردَن	fight (v.)	**mobareze kardan**
مُتأهِل	married	**mote'ahel**
مُتَّحِد	united, allied	**mottahed**
مُتَخَصِّص	specialist, expert	**motekhasses**
مُتفاوت	different	**motefaavet**
مُتَوَلِّد	born (n.)	**motevalled**
مِثال	example	**mesaal**
مِثل	like	**mesl**
مَثَلاً	for example	**masalan**
مُجازات	punishment	**mojaazaat**
مُجَرَّد	single, unmarried	**mojarrad**
مُجرِم	criminal	**mojrem**
مُچ	wrist	**moch**
مُحاکِمه	trial	**mohaakeme**
مُحَقِّق	researcher	**mohaghghegh**
مَحَل	location, place	**mahal**
مَحَلّه	neighborhood	**mahalle**
مَحلول	solution	**mahlool**
مَحَلّی	local	**mahallee**
مَخصوص	special	**makhsoos**
مِداد	pencil	**medaad**
مُدَّت	period, duration	**moddat**
مَدرِسه	school	**madrese**
مُدیر	manager, director, principal	**modeer**
مُدیریَت	management	**modeereeyat**

مَذهَب	religion	**mazhab**
مَذهَبی	religious	**mazhabee**
مُرَبّا	jam, jelly	**morabbaa**
مَربوط	related	**marboot**
مَرد	man	**mard**
مُرداد	5th month of the Persian calendar	**mordaad**
مَردُم	people	**mardom**
مُردَن	die (v.)	**mordan**
مُرده	dead	**morde**
مِرسی	thanks	**mersee**
مَرطوب	humid, moist	**martoob**
مُرغ	chicken	**morgh**
مُرغابی	(wild) duck	**morghaabee**
مَرکَز	center	**markaz**
مَرکَزی	central	**markazee**
مَریض	sick, patient	**mareez**
مَریضی	sickness, disease	**mareezee**
مَریَم	Miriam, feminine name	**maryam**
مَزارِع	farms	**mazaare'**
مُزد	wage	**mozd**
مَزرَعه	farm	**mazra'e**
مِس	copper	**mes**
مَسئول	responsible	**mas'ool**
مَسئولیَت	responsibility	**mas'ooleeyat**
مُسابِقه	match, competition	**mosaabeghe**
مُساوی	equal	**mosaavee**
مُستَقِل	independent	**mostaghel**
مَسجِد	mosque	**masjed**
مَسکَن	housing	**maskan**
مُسَکِّن	pain killer	**mosakken**
مُسَلسَل	machine gun	**mosalsal**
مُسَلمان	Muslim	**mosalmaan**
مَسیحی	Christian (adj.)	**maseehee**
مَسیحیَت	Christianity	**maseeheeyat**
مَسیر	path	**maseer**
مُشابه	similar	**moshaabeh**
مُشارِکَت	participation	**moshaarekat**
مُشارِکَت کَردَن	participate (v.)	**mosharekat kardan**
مُشت	fist, fistful	**mosht**
مُشتَرَک	joint, in common	**moshtarak**
مَشروب	alcoholic drinks	**mashroob**
مَشروط	conditional	**mashroot**
مُشکِل	problem, issue	**moshkel**
مُشکِلات	problems	**moshkelaat**
مِشکی	black	**meshkee**
مُصاحِبه	interview	**mosaahebe**
مُصاحِبه کَردَن	interview (v.)	**mosaahebe kardan**
مَصرَف	consumption	**masraf**
مَصرَف کُنَنده	consumer	**masraf konande**
مَصرَف گَرایی	consumerism	**masrafgaraayee**
مُصَمَّم	determined	**mosammam**
مَطبوعات	press (n.)	**matboo'aat**
مُطَلَّقه	divoced (woman)	**motallaghe**
مُطمَئِن	certain, sure	**motma'en**
مُعادِل	equivalent	**mo'aadel**
مَعبَد	temple	**ma'bad**
مِعده	stomach	**me'de**
مُعَرِّفی	introduction	**mo'arrefee**
مُعَرِّفی کَردَن	introduce (v.)	**mo'arrefee kardan**
مُعَلِّم	teacher, instructor	**mo'allem**
مَعمولاً	usually	**ma'moolan**
مَعنی	meaning	**ma'nee**
مُغَذّی	nutritious	**moghazzee**
مَغز	brain	**maghz**
مَقاله	article, paper	**maghaale**
مُقایسه	comparison	**moghaayese**
مُقایسه کَردَن	compare (v.)	**moghaayese kardan**
مُکافات	punishment, trouble	**mokaafaat**
مَگَس	fly (n.)	**magas**
مُمکِن	possible	**momken**
مَمنون	thankful, thanks	**mamnoon**
مَن	I, me	**man**
مُناسِب	suitable, fitting	**monaaseb**
مَناطِق	regions, areas	**manaategh**

مُنتَشِر کَردَن	publish (v.)	montasher kardan
مُنتَظِر	waiting (adj.)	montazer
مَنزِل	home	manzel
منشأ	source	mansha'
مَنطَقه	region, area	mantaghe
مِنو	menu	meno
مِه	fog	meh
مِه آلود	foggy	mehaalood
مَهدِکودَک	daycare center	mahdekoodak
مُهر	stamp, seal	mohr
مِهر	7th month of the Persian calendar, kindness, love	mehr
مُهر زَدَن	stamp (v.)	mohr zadan
مُهر و موم	sign and seal	mohr o moom
مِهرَبان	kind	mehrabaan
مو	hair, grapevine	moo, mo
مُواظِب	careful	movaazeb
موبایل	cell phone	mobaayl
موتور	motorcycle, motor, engine	motor
موتورسیکلت	motorcycle	motorseeklet
موجود	existing	mojood
مُوَرِّخ	historian	movarrekh
مورد	case	mored
موز	banana	moz
موسیقی	music	mooseeghee
موش	mouse	moosh
موضوع	topic	mozoo'
مُوَفَّق	successful	movaffagh
مُوَفَّقِیَت	success	movaffagheeyat
میدان	field, square, circle	meydaan
میز	table, desk	meez
میلیارد	billion	meelyaard
میلیون	million	meelyoon
میمون	monkey	meymoon
مینا	Mine, feminine name	meenaa
میوه	fruit	meeve

ن

ناب	pure	naab
نابَرابر	unequal	naabaraabar
نادان	unwise	naadaan
نادِر	rare	naader
نارنجی	orage (adj.)	naarenjee
نارِنگی	tangerine	naarengee
نام	name	naam
نامِ خانِوادِگی	surname	naam e khaanevaadegee
نامه	letter	naame
نان	bread	naan
ناهار	lunch	naahaar
نَبَرد	battle	nabard
نَتیجه	result	nateeje
نَتیجه گیری	conclusion	nateeje geeree
نُخُست‌وَزیر	prime minister	nokhost vazeer
نَر	male	nar
نَرده	fence, railing	narde
نَرمِش	exercise	narmesh
نَرمِش کَردَن	exercise (v.)	narmesh kardan
نَزدیک	close (adj.)	nazdeek
نِژاد	race	nezhaad
نِژادپَرَست	racist	nezhaadparast
نِژادپَرَستی	racism	nezhaadparastee
نَسیم	breeze	naseem
نِشَست	sat	neshast
نِشَستَن	sit (v.)	neshastan
نَظَر	view, opinion	nazar
نَظم	order (n.)	nazm
نَفت	petroleum	naft
نَفَر	person	nafar
نَفَس کِشیدَن	breathe (v.)	nafas kesheedan
نَقّاش	painter	naghghaash
نَقّاشی	painting	naghghashee
نَقّاشی کردن	paint (v.)	naghghaashee kardan

نَقد کَردَن	cash (v.), critique (v.)	**naghd kardan**
نُقره	silver	**noghree**
نُقرهای	silver (adj.)	**nogree'ee**
نُقطه	point, dot	**noghte**
نگاه کَردَن	look (v.)	**negaah kardan**
نَمایَندِگان	representatives	**namaayandegaan**
نَمایَنده	representative	**namaayandeh**
نَمَک	salt	**namak**
نه	no	**na**
نُه	9	**noh**
نُهصَد	900	**nohsad**
نَهَنگ	whale	**nahang**
نو	new	**no**
نَوار	tape	**navaar**
نوبَت	turn (n.)	**nobat**
نَوَد	90	**navad**
نور	light	**noor**
نوزاد	newborn	**nozaad**
نوزدَه	19	**noozdah**
نوشابه	beverage	**nooshaabe**
نوشت	wrote	**nevesht**
نِوشتَن	write (v.)	**neveshtan**
نوشته	writing (n.)	**neveshte**
نوشید	drank	**noosheed**
نوشیدَن	drink (v.)	**noosheedan**
نوع	type, kind	**no'**
نُوه	grandchild	**nave**
نویسَنده	writer, author	**neveesande**
نی	straw	**ney**
نِیاز	need (n.)	**neeyaaz**
نیرو	force (n.)	**neeroo**
نیروِی دَریایی	Navy	**neeroo ye daryaayee**
نیروِی هَوایی	Air Force	**neeroo ye havaayee**
نیروِی ویژه	Special Forces	**neeroo ye veezhe**
نیست	is not	**neest**

ه

هاله	halo	**haale**
هِجدَه	18	**hejdah**
هَر	each	**har**
هَرگز	never	**hargez**
هِزار	1000	**hezar**
هِزاره	millennium	**hezaare**
هَزینه	cost, expense	**hazeene**
هَست	is, there is	**hast**
هَشت	8	**hasht**
هَشتاد	80	**hashtaad**
هَشتصَد	800	**hashtsad**
هَفت	7	**haft**
هَفتاد	70	**haftaad**
هَفتتیر	pistol	**hafteer**
هَفتصَد	700	**haftsad**
هَفتِگی	weekly	**haftegee**
هَفته	week	**hafte**
هفدَه	17	**hefdah**
هُلو	peach	**holoo**
هَم	also, too	**ham**
هَمجنسگرا	homosexual	**hamjensgaraa**
هَمچنین	also	**hamcheneen**
هَمدَست	accomplice	**hamdast**
هَمسَر	spouse	**hamsar**
هَمکار	colleague	**hamkaar**
هَمکاری	cooperation	**hamkaaree**
هَمکاری کَردَن	cooperate (v.)	**hamkaaree kardan**
هَمگانی	public	**hamegaanee**
هَمه	all, every	**hame**
هَمیشه	always	**hameeshe**
هِندِوانه	watermelon	**hendevaaneh**
هُنَر	art	**honar**
هُنَرمَند	artist	**honarmand**
هُنَری	artisitic	**honoree**
هَنوز	still, yet	**hanooz**

هَوا	air, weather	**havaa**
هَواپیما	airplane	**havaapeymaa**
هَویج	carrot	**haveej**
هیچ کَس	no one	**heech kas**
وَ	and	**va**
واحِد	unit	**vaahed**
واریز کَردَن	deposit (v.)	**vaareez kardan**
واژه	word	**vaazhe**
واقعاً	really	**vaaghe'an**
واقِعی	real	**vaaghe'ee**
واقِعیَت	reality	**vaaghe'eeyat**
وَرزِش	sport, exercise	**varzesh**
وَرزِش کَردَن	exercise (v.)	**varzesh kardan**
وَرَق	sheet	**varagh**
وُرود	entry	**vorood**
وُرودی	entrance	**voroodee**
وَزن	weight	**vazn**
وَزن کَردَن	weigh (v.)	**vazn kardan**
وَزن کَم کَردَن	lose weight (v.)	**vazn kam kardan**

وَسَط	middle	**vasat**
وَقت	time, when	**vaght**
وَلی	but	**valee**
ویژه	special	**veezhe**

ی

یا	or	**yaa**
یازدَه	11	**yaazdah**
یاس	jasmine	**yaas**
یَخ	ice	**yakh**
یَزد	Yazd (city in Iran)	**yazd**
یَعنی	it means	**ya'nee**
یِک	1	**yek**
یِکدیگَر	each other	**yekdeegar**
یِکسان	identical	**yeksaan**
یِکشَنبه	Sunday	**yekshambe**
یَهودی	Jewish	**yahoodee**
یَهودیَت	Judaism	**yahoodeeyat**
یونیفورم	uniform	**yooneeform**

Photo Credits

The following photographs are from:

"Books to Span the East and West"

Tuttle Publishing was founded in 1832 in the small New England town of Rutland, Vermont [USA]. Our core values remain as strong today as they were then—to publish best-in-class books which bring people together one page at a time. In 1948, we established a publishing outpost in Japan—and Tuttle is now a leader in publishing English-language books about the arts, languages and cultures of Asia. The world has become a much smaller place today and Asia's economic and cultural influence has grown. Yet the need for meaningful dialogue and information about this diverse region has never been greater. Over the past seven decades, Tuttle has published thousands of books on subjects ranging from martial arts and paper crafts to language learning and literature—and our talented authors, illustrators, designers and photographers have won many prestigious awards. We welcome you to explore the wealth of information available on Asia at **www.tuttlepublishing.com**.

Published by Tuttle Publishing, an imprint of Periplus Editions (HK) Ltd.

www.tuttlepublishing.com

Copyright © 2023 by Periplus Editions (HK) Ltd.

All rights reserved.

Library of Congress Control Number: 2022935356

ISBN 978-0-8048-5289-0

26 25 24 23   5 4 3 2 1

Printed in Singapore   2307TP

Distributed by

North America, Latin America & Europe
Tuttle Publishing
364 Innovation Drive
North Clarendon,
VT 05759-9436 U.S.A.
Tel: 1 (802) 773-8930
Fax: 1 (802) 773-6993
info@tuttlepublishing.com
www.tuttlepublishing.com

Asia Pacific
Berkeley Books Pte. Ltd.
3 Kallang Sector #04-01
Singapore 349278
Tel: (65) 6741-2178
Fax: (65) 6741-2179
inquiries@periplus.com.sg
www.tuttlepublishing.com

TUTTLE PUBLISHING® is a registered trademark of Tuttle Publishing, a division of Periplus Editions (HK) Ltd.